Adventures In the Holy Ghost

In Praise of

ADVENTURES IN THE HOLY GHOST

If I had to give this book an evaluation, I would give it the maximum mark allowed. My sister, Lourdes, is a God-fearing woman anointed by the Holy Spirit. I take my hat off to her. God has been pleased to grace her with many gifts—not the least of which is the gift of writing. While reading this book I was transported to the Province of Bocas del Toro, where I was born. I re-lived many experiences and remembrances of the difficulties we went through, and it brought tears to my eyes; but in the midst of everything, God has never forsaken us.

When taking this journey through The Adventures in the Holy Ghost I was impacted as I read the miracles and testimonies in each chapter. The Holy Spirit has used the Prophet Lourdes to reach the physical, emotional and spiritual needs of the people to whom she ministered on these evangelistic missions. The hardships that she endured have been used by God to bless others, thus fulfilling His purpose.

With great humility I can say that I am proud to have such an intelligent, committed sister who allows herself to be used by the Holy Spirit; because if it were not for Him, she could not accomplish such success.

If this book has come into your hands, it will be a blessing to you. Let others know about it so that they can receive the victory they need. If He did it for Lourdes, He will do it for you.

CONGRATULATIONS SISTER, AND MAY GOD CONTINUE BLESSING AND INSPIRING YOU THROUGH THE HOLY SPIRIT

– Jeronima Lewin

ADVENTURES
In the Holy Ghost

By

Lourdes Lewin

Published by
Eagles Word Christian Publisher LLC
New York

Adventures in the Holy Ghost
ISBN: 978-1-7374692-1-6

Copyright © September 2021 by Lourdes Lewin
All rights reserved. No part of this book may be reproduced, scanned, or distributed in any printed form without permission.

Most Scriptures are taken from the
King James Version of the Bible
except otherwise stated.

Printed in the United States of America.

Dedication

To my brother, Pastor Mario E. Nicolas: you have followed the principles laid down by our parents. They demonstrated unselfish love and tender care for us all. You have done the same for your family, especially for your sisters. I truly love you and feel so blessed to have a great, dedicated, loving, faithful brother like you.

I will always remember and cherish those moments when you would rise early in the morning and gather the family for devotions. Those times were uplifting and encouraging. You planted the seed of God's Word in me, and it is bearing fruit today.

I also thank God for your wife Marva Nicolas who has been a great inspiration. She has always loved and supported me. I am blessed to have two wonderful nephews: Marlo and Mario Nicolas Jr.

Acknowledgements

I exalt the Lord of my salvation who has seen me through the good and bad times. Without Him, I do not know where I would be. He has been the biggest part of my life; He is my all in all. He strengthened me when I was weak, and He picked me up when I was down. He encouraged me when I was discouraged, and much more. *"Adventures in the Holy Ghost"* is the work of the Holy Ghost in my life.

I give thanks to God for my sister Jeronima Lewin De Moulton, who has always encouraged me to use my gift of writing. She read the first chapter of my book and was convinced that it would touch many lives. She found the descriptive accounts of my journey intriguing; the narrative of each chapter eradicated any question about the authenticity of the power of God. The stories brought tears to her eyes.

I am grateful for Judy Howard, Publisher, *Eagles Word Christian Publisher LLC*; https://eaglespublisher.com. She will always be a cherished friend, who has consistently encouraged me to SOAR and reach my dreams.

Richard & Judith Manigault, Graphic Artist & CEO and Editor-in-Chief of *Link2us Magazine* have supported me on this journey in many ways. I am forever grateful. Thank you

Judith for linking me with the right professionals to see this project to its completion.

I thank God for Kae Lee, Copy Editor, *U R Destined 4 Success. LLC*.

To my Pastors, Dr. Roberto H. Robinson Sr. & Dr. Monica Robinson, *Restoration Church of Jesus Christ Apostolic International, Inc.,* who have been a great source of support and encouragement to me.

Thanks to Pastor Dahlia Thomas, a dear friend, thanks for believing that I could utilize my creativity.

A big 'shout out' to my granddaughter, Zakiyah Shaw, who read the first draft of my book, and was deeply impacted, expressing genuine accolades.

Finally, special recognition goes to Mr. Cerus Scott Davis, Manager of *For Alll-That!!! Graphic Design,* a true professional. Thank you for understanding my vision and creating an extraordinary cover for my book. Your work brought my vision to life and epitomizes the core biblical beliefs in my heart.

Foreword

I thank you, Father, for this seed which you have sown in the earth — and called her Lourdes.

Lourdes: as a seed, you have grown roots deep and wide into the soil, so deep that your roots have tapped water.

Now you are like a tree planted by the rivers of water that brings forth her fruit in due season. Your leaves also shall not wither and whatsoever you do shall prosper. All the years which you have spent going through what seemed to be trouble, you were sending roots deep into the earth. Now your top has burst forth above the ground developing trunk, leaves, branches, and you are bearing fruit.

You are a strong and solid tree. The storms of life shall not blow you down nor uproot you, because your roots are deep and wide. Your sap gives off an aroma that attracts those persons and things that are good for you. You are equipped with both defense and support.

Dr. Catherine Jeffrey
(2014)

Preface

Many Christians believe that it is important to evangelize to others—to preach the Gospel of Jesus Christ and convey what they believe. Some Christian missionaries, like myself, travel to foreign countries to evangelize. My ministries started on the subway and buses. The ultimate goal of many who evangelize is to convert non-Christians to Christianity.

The word *evangelize* comes from the Latin word *evangelizare*, meaning "to spread or preach the Gospel." The Greek root *euangelizesthai*, means "bring good news." I believe it simply means to love others enough to share the good news with them, wherever they are. Evangelizing is essential for the conversion of souls.

As an Evangelist, although you are not always welcomed by the people you are trying to reach, you must not be discouraged. If you feel the inner witness and drive to win souls for Christ, go forward and let that spirit of obedience usher you into the harvest fields. Those who win souls are God's laborers sent out on a mission. While on that mission, pray for the Lord who is in charge of the harvest to send more laborers into His field. According to Proverbs 11:30, *the fruit of the righteous is a tree of life, and he that wins souls is wise.*

This book, *Adventures in the Holy Ghost,* gives a snapshot of what this type of journey and work looks like. It enlightens as well as informs of the reality of serving Christ on the mission fields.

Table of Contents

Introduction i
Chapter 1: Growing Up on the Island 1
Chapter 2: Recognizing the Gifts Within 7
Chapter 3: Reflections 16
Chapter 4: Miracle on the Plane 18
Chapter 5: Assignment in Hawaii 22
Chapter 6: Secrets Revealed through Visions 39
Chapter 7: Healed by Faith 42
Chapter 8: Trance to Africa 44
Chapter 9: Missionary Trip to Mexico 46
Chapter 10 Dreams Become Real in Manhattan 55
Chapter 11 Ministry on the Night Train 70
Chapter 12: My Path to Europe: Netherlands 79
Chapter 13: Missionary Trip to Trinidad & Tobago . 85
Chapter 14: Ministry Trip to the Virgin Islands 87
Chapter 15: No Distance in the Spirit Realm 89
Chapter 16: Ministry Trip to Nicaragua 91
Chapter 17: My Missionary Trip to Panama 101
Chapter 18: Holy Spirit: Yesterday, Today, Forever. 103

Introduction

Adventures in the Holy Ghost is an intimate account of my spiritual journey. The stories are true accounts of adventurous, miraculous events, and are written in easy-to-read fashion. The book reveals divine interventions in my life. I am convinced that reliance on signs and visions from God manifests unexpected miracles in the lives of ordinary people. I believe that readers will be intrigued by the Godly encounters witnessed by corporate executives, supervisors, coworkers, family members, and even pastors. Many of them agree that travailing prayer, faith, and belief bring lasting victories.

As the pages unfold, I share candidly about my unforgettable childhood along the beautiful Caribbean Coast with my siblings and our protective dog Pluto, as well as my battle with asthma. My story can assist you in learning how to recognize Biblical principles, and how to apply them to help you face, endure, and manage hardships.

Enjoy the journey with me! I pray you will be blessed.

Chapter 1

Growing Up on the Island

We were the last two of seven siblings. My sister and I were born in the early '50s, two years apart. Our family lived in the Province of Bocas del Toro Archipelago, Panama — a stretch of water containing many islands off the Caribbean coast.

Isla Colon is the main island, and is known for its rich fauna, flora, and natural beauty, making it a highly regarded tourist attraction. The island is also known for its beautiful beaches and pristine waters. If you stand in the water waist-deep, you can see a rich array of fish and exotic plant life just at glance.

Growing up on the island, Jeronima (my little sister) and I did everything together. Most folks thought we were twins due to our close age proximity. We enjoyed lots of fun with our jet black dog Pluto (I never knew the type of dog he was; we were just happy to have one), but as I remember, Pluto loved swimming with us and brought us joy, friendship, and protection.

I recall an indigenous man who would pass by our house every day, and each time he passed, Pluto would bark and charge at him, each time ripping his shirt, yet the man never changed his route. I guess he liked the adventure. As a young girl growing up in the early '60s, life was carefree. I had the reputation of being mischievous and fun-loving, as I would run along the seashore with my friends and siblings.

My Sister, Pluto, and Me

Often my mother would send me on errands to the store. Like a shadow, my little sister would tag along, as well as our dog. Mom (Lorline) would tell us not to take Pluto, but as kids often do, we disobeyed, and took him anyway. We would want to bathe him, so we would take him to the dock where, for fun, my sister would throw him into the sea. On one particular day, as she pushed him, she fell in right behind him. She was soaking wet and was worried about what to do, but I assured her that I would handle the situation by taking the groceries upstairs to mom, while she stood in the sun out back to dry off. Funny! The innocent mischief of children.

Asthmatic Attack

Mom adored dressing us alike. She loved all seven of us, but paid more attention to the two of us because we were the youngest. Our other siblings were older and away at college. Having been a preemie, I needed a little more attention because I had developed asthma. I can recall one particular incident in which I had a severe asthmatic attack. Since it was a life-and-death matter, my parents, alarmed and panicky, transported me by boat on a chilly, breezy night to a faraway island where I would receive better treatment. The anxiety, tension, and fear of losing me were high; I will never forget my mother's words to Dad: "George, I think we lost her this time!" she exclaimed. "Her pupils have gone backward; only the white of her eyes are showing!" Although I was very young, (probably shy of six or seven years old), in my mind I thought to myself: 'If she feels like she is losing me *this* time, it means that it was not the first time that I was close to death.' My asthma would eventually cease due to her wisdom, love, and care. She would often use herbs to keep us well. She credited God for her unique knowledge, and often you could hear her shouting Hallelujah!!!

Being the island's herbalist was not her only shared gift. Lorline was a popular Contralto singer, and an organist. She demonstrated her talents by teaching music and singing in her father's church choir. Her gifts were something the world should have known. My mother was also a seamstress, and as such, she made our clothes, and other items such as beautifully embroidered tablecloths. Some of these item have remained as family heirlooms today. My sister inherited her creative talent of working with her hands. She was amazing.

Mama's Hardship

Childhood was not without its share of hardships, however. As time passed, we reluctantly had to leave our beautiful island to go to live with Grandpa due to mom's disability which was brought on by domestic abuse. My little sister and I adjusted to the new environment and established new friendships. Everybody knew my grandfather and my mom. So it was easy.

Catching Crawfish

We were considered poor. Yet, despite our lack of resources, we were not negatively impacted. We believed that our Dad was a good provider. We enjoyed a great childhood despite later disappointments. When I look at today's generation, I often think that they have less of a variety of fun things to do. Modern trends cause them to be absorbed in electronic games, cellphones and the internet, and old-fashioned fun may be lost. Nothing can match the joy of free-spirited swimming and climbing fruit trees, and of course, catching crawfish with soap.

My sister and I were also fortunate enough to enjoy small pleasures such as going to the river to wash our clothes and to swim. As we lived in a rural community, we did not have running water or electricity in the house, so we used kerosene lamps. Going to the river to wash was convenient because we would wash, rinse, and hang the clothes on the grass or on the tree branches to dry. While we waited, we had fun swimming in the river, playing in the streams, and climbing trees for fruit to eat. While there, we would also use large rocks to build a fire; the purpose of which was to roast the crawfish (similar to a shrimp) that we caught in the stream.

To catch the crawfish we would place soap inside of a calabash—a large, woodsy gourd from a tropical American tree that can serve as a water container. We had a half-gourd which we used to catch water, or even to drink liquids. While we were waiting for the crawfish to come down the stream, we set a piece of soap in the calabash, placed it in the bottom of the stream, and kept our feet in the water so as to not startle the little creatures. Also in the stream were groups of little fish that nibbled at our feet and gave us the best pedicures!

The Dare

As a child, I loved the water and swam and dived like a fish. We would go to the beach every day to bathe and pick up seashells and have fun. On one particular day, as I looked out at the sea, I saw a light blue, crystalline circle, which sparked my curiosity. It stood out because the rest of the water was darker. It was far from the water's edge and the docks, about the length of a city block.

My friends challenged me; they dared me to go out there and initially they did not believe that I would do it. To their great surprise, however, I decided to accept the challenge. You need to know that at the time, I was between nine and ten years old! Can you imagine the feat of courage I was about to carry out? As I swam out to the deep blue patch, I was surprised by a large school of barracuda and sawfishes grouped by age. The young ones did not seem to be dangerous, but the grown ones had long snouts called Rostrum, which looked like chain saws. What did I do, you ask? I made the fastest U-turn you can imagine and swam and dived as fast as I could until I reached the shore, cheered on by my friends.

I was so happy to make it back safely! Mom, who was back at home, had no idea of the fearless things I was doing. Thank God that my little sister who was two years younger and a good spectator, kept her mouth shut. "Mums" was the word.

Catch The Cork!!

Even then, I realize that God kept and protected us from all dangers seen and unseen; He amazes me! Without Him, I don't know where I would be today. This brings another story to mind.

I always felt a great responsibility and obligation to take care of my mother, grandfather, and little sister. All these events took place when I was nine through twelve years of age. My mom always told me that I was dependable because I was always fishing and looking for extra food to cook for the four of us. Often, I would go to the other island to purchase groceries on the only available means of transportation—a boat. It had no motor, just a paddle with which to navigate gigantic waves on a vast bed of water—with no land in sight. It sometimes took about two hours.

The route to the other island would cross a channel in which the Atlantic and Pacific Oceans met, and large ships would transit through. On one particular occasion, I remember that each time a small motorboat would pass us, it would create great waves that would cause our boat to go up and down. Suddenly, the cork which was at the bottom of the boat popped out and water began to sprout up into the air like a geyser! The canoe began to fill up quickly. The man navigating our small boat kept paddling to keep control and shouted: "catch the cork!!" I could see he was frightened; and while I didn't feel afraid, I couldn't catch the cork because if I stood up the boat would capsize. I placed my foot on the hole and the cork fell in the boat! After I secured it in its place, I began to bail out the excess water.

As we continued our journey, I was able to experience God's handiwork; the depth of the ocean was breathtaking! It seemed bottomless. I admired the dimensions and cascade of colors from the surface of the water to the deep. Only God! There is no other God besides Him.

> Isaiah 40:12 states, "*Who hath measured the waters in the hollow of his hand, and meted out heaven with the span, and comprehended the dust of the earth in a measure and weighed the mountains in scales. And the hills in a balance?* That scripture also states; "*To whom then will ye liken God? Or what likeness will ye compare unto Him?* My answer? No other God.

Chapter 2

Recognizing The Gift Within

Born With Gifts

While still young and living in Isla Colon, I used to envision things happening before they actually occurred. If I shared those dreams or visions with others, I felt that no one understood, because very often I would be labeled, particularly by adults. This was always painful. I wanted to be accepted and liked, not called out. As I grew older and became a Christian, this "seeing" would serve me well in the ministry. Being "called out" as a Christian is to be expected. I would come to learn that having visions is a divine gift, but that knowledge came only after many years. Meanwhile, as a child, being prone to visions was not a favorable experience for someone who was trying to fit in with her peers.

One day, as I was playing on my piazza with my neighbors and having fun with our dolls and kitchen set, it began to rain. The Caribbean rain is like an opened sky with heavy downpours. We all ran to the yard and bathed under the rainfall. As we sat on the piazza drying off, I had an open vision. There was a lady who was walking swiftly between the tall grass through a little walkway. As she walked, I had a vision of her falling onto her back. Her umbrella opened wide and landed on her chest in an upright position, (which seemed funny to me). I turned towards my friend and said, "that lady is going to fall flat on her back with the umbrella on her chest," and it happened! That was my first clear remembrance of having insight into future occurrences.

Midnight On Bastimentos Island

Three months after my birthday, which I celebrated in February, I remember sitting around the table after supper with my mother and my little sister. We were conversing about different things, and I asked my mom a question which caused her to ask me "Why?" I asked her what would happen to us if she were to die? At this time, she had lateral paralysis because of serious head trauma she had suffered, and could only use one hand. My response to her why was, "because now we are girls 11 and 13 years old with a sick mother." So, I told her I wanted to know, but she replied, "don't ask me that."

I was becoming sleepy, therefore I asked my mother to touch me with her cane to wake me, when she was ready to retire for the night. I then went into a spare room to lie down. What happened next was puzzling. I was sound asleep, and a vision came. In it, I envisioned my mother coming to the doorway. She lifted her cane to wake me up, but instead, she fell; and the sound of her fall woke me up. I saw her clearly, even though I was sound asleep. This was another vision. This time it frightened me.

That afternoon I told the neighbors what I had seen in the dream, and they called me a witch. One lady called me a devil and other derogatory names. I did not understand their reaction. I had never been referred to as such names. Their ignorance of the supernatural things of God prevented them from understanding what was occurring, and similarly, so did I.

That same night, near midnight, my mother did indeed attempt to wake me up, but unfortunately, the vision would come true. This was an unforgettable night on Bastimentos Island. There is no dark, like midnight on the Island called Bastimentos. Looking out, from that room, there were no streetlights. It was pitch black. I screamed with a loud voice. My agonizing, loud voice woke the neighbors. Kerosene lamps were lit. Friends and neighbors hurried to our door. They screamed back, "What's wrong Lourdes?" "What's wrong? Is your mother alright?" "No! She fell. I cannot lift her from the floor. She is cold." I knew she was gone from us. My heart ached badly.

There were first responder personnel on the island, but they were far away, upon a hill. Cousin Lin, my sister, and I (Lin was older and could run fast) met the first responders and headed back with them. However, when they arrived, my mom was pronounced dead. We were all devastated. R.I.P. Mama.

Much later in ministry, I would come to understand more about dreams and visions and the gifts of the Holy Spirit such as:

The Word of Knowledge: which brings revelation concerning things past or present.

The Word of Wisdom: which brings revelation pointing to the future, including the plan and purpose of God; and of course,

Visions: which are instruments of divine communication from God.

After my mother passed, my aunt took us to live with her in another province. We had to leave all "childish things" (meaning fun) behind. I experienced a life of trials and failures that almost put me over the edge mentally and emotionally.

I grew up with my aunt, got married at age 21 and had my firstborn, a daughter. I worked in the province for a few years as a forensic assistant. Later, I was employed by a prestigious company as a secretary for one year and then I migrated to America in the late 70's. As time went by, I gave birth to two more children.

I soon accepted Jesus Christ as my Lord and Savior, as a result of those hard times. I became born again, and since then I have experienced great adventures in the Holy Ghost.

The Disco Ball: How He Drew Me

I was older now, and in time, there was a notable void in my life. I missed Mom so much. I began looking for love in all the wrong places. I was unhappy, lonely, and confused. To fill that emptiness, I started to 'have some fun.' I realized later that there was only one Person who could satisfied that longing and that Person was JESUS.

I frequented the clubs for parties. I thought that the loud music and the crowds would quench the longing and emptiness that I felt, but it all blew right through me like a whirlwind.

I attended a party one weekend — I loved to dance. I was not involved in drinking and other things people do in clubs. That night I was feeling extremely lonely and blue, so I thought that I would feel happy if I could have some fun, but to my surprise, I felt out of place and didn't get up to dance as I usually did; instead, I began to look around at everyone dancing under the colorful flashing lights of the disco ball and found that everyone looked like puppets moving around at a fast pace.

I began to think that they looked silly, and I questioned myself as to why I was in this place. At that point I began to feel uneasy and was ready to leave. The "friends" I was with began to tell me that I was being a wallflower, and a party pooper, because they knew that I loved to dance, but not that night.

I left the club more depressed, but the unfolding of God's plan for my life was at hand; that was the night in which God drew me to His side. It did not matter that I had just arrived at the party, I could not stay.

Waking up every day seemed to me like a broken record or a revolving door. I was depressed: I had persistent feelings of sadness, and loss of interest in normal activities. As soon as my feet hit the floor, the overwhelming sadness and feelings of loneliness enveloped my entire being.

On one such morning, feeling hopeless. I cried out in desperation pointing my index finger upwards towards my ceiling and into the sky, and I uttered these words "I am tired of feeling sad and lonely! If there is a God, then please help me!" Something happened at that moment. I felt as if I was suspended in time and I prayed saying, "Lord, I need to find a church."

I took a shower and went for a walk. I became intrigued with the surroundings because I had recently moved into the neighborhood, so I walked on and stumbled upon a Methodist church. I went in, and later decided to attend their Sunday services. The lessons I learned would follow me into young adult life, and I would teach many of them to my children.

Full Gospel Church Visit

After attending that church for a while, I was invited to a Full Gospel Church. The choir sang the unforgettable song entitled, "*God Cares for You*" and this song touched every fiber in my being. I cried uncontrollably throughout the rendition and shortly thereafter I sensed a sweet, calm peace throughout my body. Feelings of profound joy overcame me, and I found myself smiling.

Looking back now, I realize that I was being set free from all of my burdens and woes. The heaviness I was experiencing was supernaturally removed and I was no longer the same on the inside. I began to study the Bible starting in the books of Isaiah, and 1st and 2nd Samuel. These became my new favorite books.

One Sunday morning during service I felt the urge to pray so I went to the altar. As I prayed, I could hear myself muttering what sounded like a foreign language. It was flowing fluently. I repeatedly shouted 'hallelujah' and my whole body shivered in unison. As I got up to leave, I became self-conscious and wondered if anyone close by had heard me and I felt a bit awkward if not fearful. I did not fully comprehend this wonderful experience, so I kept it to myself until I later learned about the Holy Spirit and speaking in tongues as mentioned in the Book of Acts.

Not too long after this experience, I had another encounter with the Holy Spirit. It was a Sunday morning, and very few people were in attendance for this particular morning class. As the lesson went on, I thought I heard someone say: "read Jeremiah One." I looked behind me to see who was speaking and saw no one. The Sunday school teacher kept on with the lesson and I heard the same voice again, so I nonchalantly ignored it until I heard it again for the third time. It finally caught my attention and immediately after the class was over I went into the choir room and took out my Bible. I found the Book of Jeremiah and read chapter one. The first five verses jumped off the pages into my soul and I lingered there reading and re-reading them.

The words of Jeremiah the son of Hilkiah, of the priests that were in Anathoth in the land of Benjamin: To whom the word of the Lord came in the days of Josiah the son of Amon king of Judah, in the thirteenth year of his reign.

It came also in the days of Jehoiakim the son of Josiah, king of Judah, unto the end of the eleventh year of Zedekiah the son of Josiah, king of Judah, unto the carrying away of Jerusalem captive in the fifth month. Then the word of the Lord came unto me, saying,

Before I formed thee in the belly, I knew thee; and before thou camest forth out of the womb I sanctified thee, and I ordained thee a prophet unto the nations. Jer. 1:1-5

It was exciting! I realized that it was God's commission to me. These are selected verses; I invite you to read the full chapter.

My First Experience with Prophecy

My first experience in prophesying was at an all-night prayer meeting that was held on Friday. As the service was coming to an end, I felt the power of the Holy Spirit prompting me to speak. The Spirit revealed this message: *"I will send you to the drylands to pour out my Spirit upon the drylands, like the tree planted by the rivers of living waters whose leaves will not wither. They will fight against you, but they will not succeed because I will be there to defend you."* It was so real. I was on the floor on my back, declaring one prophecy after the other. After all was over, we dismissed and went to our separate homes.

Following that, on Sunday, as the choir was marching up the aisle, a young girl who had attended the all-night prayer and had heard the prophecy, handed me a copy of the Sunday bulletin with excitement in her eyes! I placed it in my Bible. When I got to my seat in the choir stand, I placed my Bible under the seat, forgetting to check the bulletin. When the time for the announcements came, I took out the bulletin, and OH!!! I was in awe! Guess what? The design on the cover of the bulletin reflected the prophecy that had been given at the prayer meeting.

The illustration was of a cracked-up, dry parched desert land and on it was written "Soul." There was a river flowing through the land and on the water was written "the Word of God." Beside the river was a fruitful green tree. We were all amazed at God's awesomeness. This was the reason the young girl was so excited, because she knew it was God manifesting in a mighty way. Special note: The prayer meeting took place at the home of an intercessor; the pastor was not present, and the church usually makes up their bulletins early in the week so we can have it ready for Sunday.

Two years later I went to Jamaica on a missionary trip with one of the intercessors who had migrated from there, and the power of the Lord manifested even more. We went out to a central park in downtown Jamaica where we began to minister, distributing tracts and bibles. Some individuals started a riot. Someone accused us of being devils, and this led us to believe that she was mentally challenged. A large crowd gathered, and people came out to assault us with sticks, stones, and other weapons. I was a new Christian, just getting acquainted with the things of God, therefore, the only thing I knew to say was "The Blood of Jesus and Hallelujah!" and these were my two weapons.

There was a roar from the people approaching us in the park. I closed my eyes because I did not want to see when they would lift their weapon to hurt me. We held hands and prayed out loud saying, "Jesus, Jesus!" and "Hallelujah!" The next thing I knew, the roar ceased, the people dispersed, and we were unharmed. When we got back to the house where we were staying, the Lord said to me, "the prophecy has been fulfilled." I asked, "Lord, what prophecy?" He reminded me that in 1985 He assured me that they will fight against me, but they will not succeed. This is also in the first chapter of Jeremiah, which He spoke audibly to me when He told me to read Jeremiah 1!

What an amazing God we serve!

Ministering to children in Jamaica

Chapter 3

Reflections

The Holy Spirit Manifested

I was preparing my evening meal in the kitchen, when the Lord reminded me of a miracle that had taken place at one of the local hospitals in Jamaica, West Indies. Before I tell the story, I would like to explain how God and His angels move upon the declaration of His Word. It is not always in the long prayers that He answers or manifests His power, but in the declaration and decree. Sometimes, we want to feel the witness of His presence, and if we do not feel or rather sense His presence, we think He is not involved. On the contrary, wherever we are, the Holy Spirit is, and He is ready to manifest Himself in the situation. *"And thou shalt decree a thing and it shall be established unto thee: and the light shall shine upon thy ways"* Job 22:28.

Miracle at the Hospital

A Simple Prayer of Declaration

I was visiting Jamaica, West Indies, on a missionary trip to distribute toys and clothes to people in need. While there, we decided to visit my friend's mother who was hospitalized at the time.

As we were visiting with her, the pastor with whom I was associated sent for me to visit another patient who was in another ward down the hall. When I arrived at her room, they asked me to pray for her. There were about five of us plus the patient in the room, for a total of six persons, and we were in one accord. Before I prayed, I asked her what her request was, and she explained that she would be undergoing major surgery the following day. The doctors told her that she would never walk again. Both of her legs would be amputated due to a medical diagnosis. This was unimaginable and certainly very difficult to hear.

We held hands around her bed and the pastor asked me to pray. I will be honest; I felt dry, dry, dry! There was no anointing to pray for this desperate woman, but I trusted the God of my salvation. I held hands with the sisters and placed my other hand on top of the sheet that covered her entire body. I proceeded to pray a simple prayer of declaration. "I declare this lady be healed, in the name of Jesus!" After praying, under the unction of the Holy Spirit, I told her that she will definitely wear her shoes again and will walk again. And I left the room.

The following day, we went back to visit with my friend's mother, and as we walked down the corridors, we passed by the room of the other patient for whom we had prayed the day before. We observed that the bed was made up, the window opened, and a refreshing breeze was blowing the curtain. We had no time to think about what happened.

We continued our walk down the corridor, when a nurse hastily rushed towards us with a message. She reported that the patient wanted me to know that the moment I placed my hand on her legs on top of the sheet, she felt fire rush up from her legs to her neck, and the following morning after being re-examined she was discharged, and got out of bed and walked out of the hospital wearing her shoes. To say the least, the doctors were amazed by this miracle! That is why we did not see her in her room when we passed by. No amputation was necessary! God performed a miracle! All I did was to declare His Word and all of us agreed in prayer. The effectual fervent prayer of the righteous avails much. Glory to God!

Chapter 4

Miracle On the Plane

God Raised the Dead

Upon arrival at the terminal, I saw her; a well-dressed, attractive woman, who looked somewhat familiar. She stood out to me and seemed to be everywhere every time I looked up. We finally boarded the plane back to New York; it wasn't a full flight. I took my seat on the plane next to the window, and to my amazement, her seat was in my row.

I did not know her personally, but I remembered growing up in the province where her family lived, so I began to talk to her and asked about former classmates. She responded with information about them.

Running From the Death Angel

As we talked, I asked her about her trip, and she shared with me that her trip had not been pleasant. Death seemed to be snatching family members in their early 30's, and there had been several deaths in the family over a short period of time. On this occasion she had traveled to attend a funeral, and the following day after that funeral, as she was on her way to the airport to fly back to New York, she had to turn right around, because another family member had passed away, and she had to stay for yet another funeral—scary!

This was devastating, and I felt impressed to tell her that it was a death angel running rampant through her family snatching all the young family members, and that she had to be careful that she would not be the next victim. I also asked her about her faith because she needed to get connected with the Lord. She said she was a Believer, so I prayed with her and rebuked the death angel. We exchanged contact information and continued on our journey. In all of this, I felt that the Lord would be magnified.

The Next Phase Is Staggering

Originally, when I had boarded the plane, after settling in I looked around to see who was behind me. In the section where we were seated there were about four people. Directly behind us was a medical student with a stethoscope around his neck; in front of us was one person, and to our left, one person; and we were seated on the right side of the plane. In this whole section there were only five of us. I relaxed and got ready to enjoy the flight.

Right after takeoff, I had a snack and turned on the TV. Now to be specific, the lady was seated in the aisle seat in our row. I was at the window seat, and there was no one between us. I spent some time looking out of the window but soon fell asleep. Somehow, I was sensing a prompting to look around; however, I soon dozed off again. There was a song in my heart, so with eyes closed, I began to hum it. I began to feel the volume of the song increase within me, and I realized that God was trying to get my attention! I opened my eyes and happened to look around, and to my surprise it looked as if the lady was stretching out her arm towards me. It seemed that she had been trying to get my attention for some time, but as we were seated so far apart, she was not able to touch me. I suppose she had no strength to get up out of her seat to wake me up.

Without hesitation I reached and grabbed her hand, and exclaimed "WOW!" Her hand was as cold as ice. She told me that she was seeing herself going through a dark tunnel; and then she faded out again. This confirmed to me that she had been struggling for some time before I became aware.

The lady fainted. I did not scream or make a scene, but I asked urgently for someone to call for help. The stewardess hurried toward us and asked if there were any doctors on the plane. No one came forward. They asked the medical student, who was seated behind us to take her vitals. The lady had no pulse, but he kept checking. However, there was no sign of life. We then lifted all the handles of the empty seats between us, and we stretched her out. Still, there was no sign of life. Finally, they brought grey blankets and covered her. She was as cold as a block of ice. I was still sitting near the lady, unsure of what to do. We were all very disturbed. I listened for God's directions.

God's Instruction to Me

He said, *"Don't Leave Her Side."* They laid her out with her head toward the window and legs facing the aisle. I went into the aisle at her feet, and began to pray until we were descending into New York. She had fainted a little after we had taken off, and our flight lasted over four hours, so you can imagine.

In my mind I knew that she was dead, and everyone who was around her knew that too. The male steward began to question me accusingly, asking me what I had done to her. Previous to her episode she had told me that should anything happen to her, to feel free to look into her pocketbook, because all her information was there. However, I did not need to do that.

When the stewardess further accused me, righteous indignation rose in me and I began to let them know as they surrounded me, that life is short and if they didn't know Jesus as Lord and Savior, this was the time to do so, and to get their life together; I was intense with my speech. They listened and walked away leaving me alone. To think of it, I don't know if there were any Federal agents on the plane, or why they acted as if I was a suspect.

I did just what the Lord commanded me to do; and stayed at her feet and prayed with her for the duration of the flight and just before we landed, she moved and opened her eyes. We sat her up and of course now here comes the stewardess with juice for her. They asked her a few medical questions such as: 'do you have diabetes, hypertension, or heart disease?' to which she responded "No." She had a complete physical before her travel to Panama and had a good bill of health. Only God!! They then informed her that they had requested a wheelchair to take her off the plane and to escort her to an ambulance which was awaiting her arrival.

Her Response

"No!! I am not taking any wheelchair or ambulance, because I was dead, and now I am alive!! I will walk off this plane the way I walked on." She thanked God for sending me as an angel to be with her in her time of need and we went our separate ways.

She would later call all of her family members from near and far—from London to Europe, to share her miraculous experience. It was around Thanksgiving at that time, so she gathered with all her family members and relatives to feast. I was honored that she invited me to attend as well, because my presence there would back up her story. I also added that God is the only One who gets **all** the Glory for what He did in her life. I am grateful. God is Awesome, Amazing and Faithful! Words are not adequate to describe HIM! Amen!

Chapter 5

My Assignment in Hawaii

In this encounter, God proved to me that He desires to bless His people. When we think He does not hear our faintest cry, our intimate petition, He in fact hears and acts upon them. I was reminded of these words.

Thus saith the LORD to his anointed, to Cyrus, whose right hand I have holden, to subdue nations before him; and I will loose the loins of kings, to open before him the two leaved gates; and the gates shall not be shut;

I will go before thee, and make the crooked places straight: I will break in pieces the gates of brass, and cut in sunder the bars of iron: And I will give thee the treasures of darkness, and hidden riches of secret places, that thou mayest know that I, the LORD, which call thee by thy name, am the God of Israel. (Isaiah 45:1-3).

He also said He will give us the desires of our heart:

Psalm 37:4 - Delight thyself also in the LORD, and He shall give you the desires of your heart.

I Had a Plan

We may plan, but God determines our steps. *Proverbs 16:9—we can make plans, but the Lord determines our steps*. My desire has always been to go to Hawaii, and to go on a cruise. In 2002 when my church sponsored a cruise to Hawaii, I thought it was the perfect combination—right up my 'alley' of desires. Three hundred fifty members planned to go on the trip, which we hoped would be the greatest adventure of our lives.

Every Minor Detail Is Important

I started to pack my luggage — separating the important documents I would need for Customs. I had to take a photo of my passport for the trip organizer and separate my green card from the passport. I stored my green card securely in a desk drawer. The following morning, in my haste to get ready for the trip, I forgot to retrieve the green card from the drawer (in which I had placed it). I left the house on the way to the airport unaware of this fact.

We boarded the plane from JFK to Salt Lake City. The flight was excellent, except for the moment when we had to fill out customs forms. I realized then that I did not have the green card and I became very nervous. I communicated the situation to the minister in charge who assured me that it was ok, no problem, nothing to fear.

There Is a Purpose in Disappointment

We arrived at Salt Lake City airport to board a larger plane to Honolulu. It took us several minutes to take off because the plane was too heavy. The crew needed to empty fuel to make it lighter. While we waited patiently, they attempted about four different times to take off. Eventually, it took off, still feeling very heavy. During the flight the plane was shaking violently making a very loud noise. I felt very scared because it felt as if it were about to split in half. I began to look around to see the reactions of the other passengers. They sat up like soldiers, unafraid. The Lord spoke to me audibly and said, "If you don't trust me now, when are you going to trust me?" I responded, "Lord I am in your hands." At that moment I looked through the window and beheld the beautiful blue waters below. I knew I had come to rest in the Lord.

Arrival in Honolulu

There were over 350 people on board the plane, and we lined up at the pier. What an exciting moment on a beautiful Sunday evening in Honolulu! I was so happy that my dream was coming to pass! Suddenly that dream was shattered. Why? Well, remember the green card securely left at home? I had needed it to board the ship because we were going to cruise in foreign waters. There were coastal police checking the ship for documents. Even though I had my passport, it was not enough, because I did not have a visa stamped in it. If I had a visa and not the green card I could have boarded, but I had neither one. Tours had been scheduled for us for every island on the itinerary.

What Happened Next

Naturally, I was not permitted on the vessel. I was left behind. Those words "left behind" haunted me. They reminded me of the reference to Christians who would miss the rapture. Night came, and I was still at the port of authority being questioned. I was being advised to go back to New York. Of course, I refused. I informed the authorities that I had paid over two thousand dollars for my trip. "I am not going back." Even though I was in a strange land all by myself, I grabbed a taxi to a hotel and got a room. It was frightening, being alone. By then, I was hungry and tired. My discouragement would last into the long hours of the night. It was not a good feeling.

Arrival at the Hotel

After I had checked in, I went to bed but could not sleep. I was weary and tormented by the words "left behind." The devil had me stressed for a period during the night. I felt tormented. All I kept hearing was that I was left behind. I felt that if I returned to New York the following day, I would perish in the plane. A whole lot of things bombarded my mind. Finally, I had enough. Despite my weakened state of mind and body I began to fight back. I repeated scriptures to counteract those negative thoughts. I knew I had been purchased with the Blood of Jesus. As a child of God, I was convinced that there is no weapon formed against me that could prosper, in Jesus' name! I kept confessing the scriptures until morning.

The next day I arrived at the embassy located in downtown Honolulu to try to get a temporary visa as previously advised. After going through the process, I was so happy that the visa was approved even though it cost me all of the money I had left. I went ahead and finalized it.

Finally, I arrived at the airport and boarded the plane to Hilo to meet up with the ship. Fortunately, the minister had stayed in touch with me. He advised me to get a taxi and meet the ship at the pier. As the plane landed, I rushed to gather my luggage. While on my way the minister reminded me that the port captain cannot allow the ship to wait, because of their set schedule. I heard several drivers saying, "taxi ma'am?" "taxi ma'am?" — it was annoying. I did not want a taxi, I just wanted to board the ship. I was still very heartbroken. The minister continued to try to console me. I feared that I would miss the voyage again. Despondent, the tears flowed. Here I was on another island stranded, at least so I thought.

The White Van Under the Palm Tree

When I exited the baggage section with my luggage and looked out, I observed a white van in the distance under a palm tree. After I realized that I may not be able to meet the ship, I got into the taxi and headed to the pier. As soon as I got there, the ship began drifting away from the pier. I could not control my emotions. "No! No!" I screamed. I was deeply disappointed and could not hold back the tears.

The same white van that I saw when I came out of the airport, belonged to the same man in the airport who was asking me if I wanted a taxi. He was the husband of the driver in the white van. I believe he saw me upset and sent his wife to pick me up. In light of the situation, I began to examine my soul and mind to see if there was something wrong with me that was causing all of these mishaps.

The Taxi Ride to the Pier

The driver, Candi Marie, was very pleasant, and somehow kept me distracted. She saw how distraught I was. She questioned me about the nature of my trip as she drove through the street with trees canopying overhead. It was a beautiful view, but I needed to get to the pier. I asked her if she could speed up a bit and she so sweetly assured me that I will meet the ship. The ride seemed like an eternity; finally, we arrived at the pier only once again, to see the ship cruising away! In my desperation, I asked two silly questions: "Can we get a boat so we can chase the ship? Can we charter a helicopter so I could be lowered down the ladder on the ship?" After all, the ship did not appear to be moving quickly. It looks like it was still close to the pier. Somehow, seeing the humor in it all, I laughed and started to sing, feeling like Gilligan on an island. It was better than being hysterical.

There was an office at the pier, so I tried to contact the port manager to seek help; but was unable to locate him. Evening was approaching by this time, and soon it would be dark. Thankfully, the taxi driver waited on me the entire time, and even invited me to sit in her van while waiting for the manager. My concerns became stronger because now I wondered how I would pay the lady for all the hours she waited for me, even turning off her meter while I waited for the port manager. As I sat there, she watched me broken, discouraged, stressed, frustrated, and worried. Besides, the night before I had not slept a wink.

The Reason I Missed the Cruise

While we sat in the car, she began to encourage me to calm myself. So, we began to pray. At that moment, I prayed with such authority. The Holy Spirit began to pray through me regarding tumors, cancer growths, depression, and other ailments. At this point, I felt the **dunamis** power of God all over us. This helped me to forget all of my problems. The **power of God** filled the vehicle. Eventually, feeling the presence of God, the lady began to laugh very loudly.

She explained the reason she was laughing, and this was her story… "You did not miss the ship once, but twice just for me!" I looked at her in amazement. She explained that the prayer I prayed, was concerning her. She had stage four cancer and had already had a partial hysterectomy. She suffered deep black periods of depression. She had no one to confide in because her husband was the pastor of her church and minster's wives were not at liberty to be transparent about their problems in the church. Therefore, she kept all of her sufferings to herself, as many do today. What she said to me next really changed my attitude forever. She revealed to me that due to her sufferings in silence she presented the Lord with a petition. Her petition was "God please send me an intercessor" and here I was, an appointed intercessor from New York, whom God sent for her. She was so grateful to God because He answered her secret prayer. We worshipped God in that van. We knew that the Almighty answers the prayers of His children.

Answered Prayers

At this point, I realized that this trip was not the grand vacation that I dreamed of, but it was a great adventure from God. He reached a woman of God, a faithful servant, who prayed to her Father in Heaven for someone to help her, and He sent me.

I had been blinded by my sorrowful state, but when the reason was revealed to me, my woes turned into an unexplainable joy. It gave me strength. The Bible says this, *"We can make plans, but God orders our steps" Proverbs: 16:9 (NLT).*

After waiting so long without results from the pier manager, this lady showed me such kindness, by giving me all the money she had made for the day driving the taxi. She had visited a street fair that day and they gave her a soda and a sandwich, and she gave that to me.

I was privileged to a personal tour of the Island of Hilo, which was exciting. She then took me to purchase food for the night. Her best friend owned a hotel, and they treated me to the best suite for the night free of charge. She was a total stranger to me, but not to God. He knew who she was and what her deepest needs were. In her secret closet, she cried out to her Heavenly Father, who loved her so much to bring me from New York, across the oceans and skies to meet this woman of God, and she in turn showered me with such kindness like I had never received before.

This kindness was also God's reward of love and faithfulness to me after I felt so devastated because of disappointment and the broken dream. It was not about my dreams or desires, but about His everlasting love towards people. He is truly an amazing God and Father.

My Trip Back to Honolulu

God did not abandon me in a strange place, but He taught me a valuable lesson. I felt like a missionary, because I was on a mission for the Lord, whether I knew it or not. I felt such an honor to have been used by God for such a mighty task. I was headed to Honolulu to meet my new sister and brother in the Lord, Pastors Cristobal and Aurora.

Candi Marie used her sky miles and got me on a flight back to Honolulu, where I was warmly received by the pastors and church members. Candi Marie and the two pastors in Honolulu would welcome me on my next ministry trip. Oh what love!!!

After my arrival back in Honolulu, I was provided a place to stay for several days, in the huge church.

While my fellow church members were still touring on the cruise ship, God had these Pastors Cris, Aurora, and the new contacts, to ensure that all my needs were met. The pastor himself would come to the church every morning to pick me up. He would even make me breakfast. Some of the members would give me a tour around the whole island, and he made sure to give them money to take me to dinner every evening. The sites included the Dole Pineapple plantation and a helicopter flight to see a waterfall that cannot be seen except from the sky. It was very impressive. The open markets aligning the waterfront turned into an escapade, and provided an ideal way to keep me busy until the time when the ship would return from cruising seven days later.

Pastors who Hosted me in Hawaii

Another Miraculous Move of God

Exhausted, I thought my mission was over, but not so! There was another miraculous move of God. It was July 4th, and the island planned to celebrate. The youth pastor and all the young people took me on a picnic. We watched the fireworks. It was amazing because we had a close-up view of creative fireworks while overlooking the waters. This was my first experience watching the Fourth of July fireworks; even though I lived in New York. I had never attended any such event previous to this one.

Fireworks in Hawaii

During the daytime, we sat on the beach enjoying the sunshine, cool breezes, and nice food that we barbecued. After all of this, the Lord instructed me to share the Word with the youth. There were many beautiful young people, and they sat in a semi–circle in front of me. In the middle of teaching, I heard the LORD say to me "Call Mary Marie" (I will use the name, Mary Marie, for privacy). With the Bible opened in my hand, I felt like I went into a trance. I picked up my cell phone and dialed the number. She answered with a casual hello. I asked her if she was ok. I had tried reaching her before I left home for my ministry trip. As we talked briefly, she acknowledged that she had heard all of my messages. I proceeded to ask a second time "are you ok?" I felt she was not being honest with me; then she shared the following with me.

At the very moment I dialed her number, she was in danger. She was about to end her life with cocktails, some scissors, or a knife. She said that if one thing did not work, she would use the other instrument to complete the job.

She said all her windows were covered with black bags and she jammed her door shut so no one could enter her room. Later, I would learn that her mother and other family members were also trying to reach her. She explained that she had prayed just before she attempted to take her life. She said she uttered these words while the knife was in one hand and the scissor in the other. She prayed, "God if you don't want me to do this, stop me!" She said that simultaneously as the words left her lips, my phone call came in! I was in shock, but God knew!! She is alive and well until now, and right after that she met her future husband and is happily married.

When God's assignment was carried out and I came back from the trance, the young people were still seated in front of me quietly, waiting on me. This was what they shared with me. They said, "you went away somewhere; your eyes looked far away; you dropped the Bible and picked up the phone and called, not saying anything to us." I believed I was moving in slow motion when I made the call without excusing myself from the group. I explained what happened, stating that not acting right away could have caused her to take her life. After that, we enjoyed a great 4th of July on the beach.

When The Ship Returned

I made sure to wait at the pier before the ship arrived. I was making sure I did not miss it again. It had been a week now. I was ready to join the crew. We would spend four extra days on land. It was a great adventure to walk out of the hotel into the water.

My Dilemma

The kindness of my friend Joy

With all that went down, I was left without money; so my church sisters and friends (mainly my friend Joy), continued to help me while on our trip. She made sure that all my needs were met. They were all glad to reconnect with me when they got off the ship in Honolulu, but Joy and I had bonded many years prior. I had rented a place from her when my children were younger, so we were not only neighbors but had developed an amazing friendship. Now, being in Honolulu together, we looked forward to traveling back home with each other. I found great pleasure in thanking those who had helped me for their kindness and support. My prayer for them was that God would continue to overflow their lives with blessings. The scripture states *"When we give to the poor, we lend to God."*

The Assault of the Enemy

Each time God does great work in the life of someone, the devil attacks the one whom God used. We still win!! Here is the story.

I went through many challenging experiences from the time I boarded the plane — being separated from the group; the lonely, sad warfare night in the hotel after the ship sailed without me; the trip to the embassy; the disappointment of twice not making it in time to connect with the ship; and I cannot forget the long wait at the pier for the manager and a pass to go back to Honolulu; the overnight stay in Hilo which was arranged by the pastors who picked me up from the airport, and my return trip to Honolulu when God provided two pastors to host my stay until the ship returned.

After all these experiences, I still encountered more rejection. Among the Christians with us was a tired-looking passenger. She got off the ship and headed towards me. She pointed her fingers into my face and screamed, "Something is wrong with you! You need to go and repent! Seek God's face and examine yourself for sure! Something is very wrong with you! You were the only one left behind!" I was shaken up, embarrassed and nervous, because here were those words again — "left behind" which tormented me. For a moment, the deranged church lady's words caused me to recall what I had previously heard so often as a child from people who were uneducated in the things of God: "You are a witch," they would exclaim very loudly.

The Sovereignty of God

He is Faithful

Psalm 104:1-2: Bless the LORD O my soul! O LORD my God, you are very great! With splendor and majesty, covering yourself with light as a garment, stretching out the heavens like a tent (ESV).

Definition of Sovereignty of God: being the ultimate source of *all* power, authority, and everything that exists.

Revelation 21:6 states: and He said unto me, it is done. I am Alpha and Omega, the beginning, and the end. I will give unto Him that is a thirst of the fountain of the water of life freely.

I experienced God's faithfulness during the special assignment in Hawaii, which at first seemed like a great mishap with tremendous disappointment, but God!!

The Great Reward

For many years, one of my greatest desires, besides going on a cruise to Hawaii, was to possess a black pearl. These pearls, from what I gathered, were rare. I was informed that Hawaii has real pearls. One of my friends advised me to choose the ugliest or most undesirable oyster and maybe I will find one.

There was a market in town, so I went there. I saw an "off-the-beat" shop with a display of pearls, so I went in. In there I saw a container with oysters, so I selected the first crusty one. The salesperson sliced the meat and pressed the oyster towards me, and out came my black pearl!! The sales personnel began to celebrate with me saying that I was a lucky person because they never experienced getting a black pearl before.

I chose another oyster and out came a gray pearl! The sales personnel began to celebrate me again! When I say celebrate, they had instruments on which they played a chanting rhythm. In addition, the sizes of the pearls were also larger than the ones on display. They reiterated that I was lucky because they had never seen any colored pearls, much less those larger sizes. This was as exciting for them as it was for me.

They also had a showcase with jewelry; therefore, with their help, I selected a pendant. They suggested a cute oyster golden pendant and set the pearl in it. It was a delicate job, but they had the necessary equipment. The cost for all of this was only $18.00; which included the oyster, pendant and the setting. I assured them that I was not dealing with luck, but it was God, who is faithful, and was rewarding me and giving me the desires of my heart to cheer me up.

A couple of days after this experience we all returned safely to our respective homes in New York. I felt greatly blessed.

Isn't He a compassionate and loving Father who loves us with an everlasting, unconditional love? Do you believe it? Hallelujah! I just couldn't keep this testimony of God's compassion, love, faithfulness, and care for me to myself, after all I went through.

Hawaiian Black Pearl

Loving People, Respecting Traditions

After my return to New York, and up until the present time, I stayed in touch with my new friends from Hawaii. At one point it seemed I had lost communication with Candi Marie and I became concerned, but found out that she was on another island teaching at the school.

Time passed and I received news that the cancer had returned aggressively and eventually she lost the battle. She went home to be with the Lord. We had met on a mission trip. I had never met anyone so passionate about loving people in the way she did. I learnt the importance of understanding culture and traditions from her. She believed in honoring the home of those to whom we ministered. I want to believe she is in the arms of our Lord. When I learnt the sad news of her death, I called immediately to encourage the family. Her husband, being a pastor, was at peace as he watched her suffering come to an end. He shared with me that the night she was transitioning the dogs were barking all night, and to him, it was a sign that it was the end.

Candi was very kind and full of God's love for people. Sleep in peace (SIP) my sister! When we do what the Lord wants, He will give us our heart's desire. Psalm 37:4 reminds us, *Delight yourself in the LORD, and He will give you the desires of your heart (ESV)*. Here we see that Candi petitioned God to send an intercessor; despite her trials she delighted herself in Him and waited patiently. When I think of it, I must exclaim "GOD is Awesome!" I cannot find a word that is grand enough to describe Him. My heart is enlarged with love, gratitude, and delight to have Him as my God and me His child. *Psalm 144:15 Happy are the people who are in such a state; Happy are the people whose God is the Lord! (NLT)*.

I could not describe what I am feeling right now as I pen these beautiful accounts. I exhort you as you read these experiences and testimonies to open your heart to the Great and Mighty God, Creator of the Universe, who made us in His image and His likeness for, without Him, nothing was made. *John 1:3 states: All things were made by Him, and without him was not anything made that was made.*

Always remember that God will select you to carry out an assignment and, because it may seem strange and impossible, you may question His directive, but you were chosen because He trusts and knows that you are able and equipped to do it.

Here is God's desire or will for mankind according to II Peter 3:9 *The Lord is not slack concerning his promise, as some men count slackness; but is long suffering to us-ward, not willing that any should perish, but that all should come to repentance.* He will go to any length to reach one soul. *The eyes of the LORD are upon the righteous, and his ears are open unto their cry. Psalm 34:15.*

God Bless!

Chapter 6

Secrets Revealed Through Visions

It's A Girl! Kiyomi Abreu

This next story is shared by the parents of the child. I want to give you a tip on how amazing God is. I was sitting one day at my computer, and suddenly I saw a vision of a beautiful baby girl floating in front of my face like on a magic carpet. She was dressed in pink, had black, soft, curly hair and a beautiful complexion. I asked, "Lord, what's this about?" He answered "Amanda's baby." I forgot all about it until it came back to my memory on the day of their marriage, and I shared it with Amanda. This was the vision of a baby girl that would be born of her.

Amanda wrote: It all started with a vision, and it sure turned into reality for us. My husband and I had just gotten married and were enjoying our new-found life together. We talked about kids without knowing how soon, but one woman did. She called me a few weeks after we had gotten married and told me God showed her our daughter. In disbelief, I said to her 'I'm not pregnant.' She told me not now but very soon. I told my husband; we looked at each other and mutually stated "yeah, right." She was very detailed about how she would look as well—'brown skin, curly hair, and very beautiful' she described. We said, "How does she even know we will have a girl? Only God can determine that."

Amanda continued, "we went about our lives as normal ignoring the information we were given. Two months down the road we took a test and came to find out we were pregnant. We both looked at each other and were still in disbelief. I immediately called Lourdes and told her. All she said to me that day was "To God be the Glory." We still told ourselves maybe it was a lucky guess....newly married; it's common to have a baby right after. Now what we were curious about was gender. She did tell us a beautiful girl. She even came to my job and gifted me a pair of socks in pink with the words "I love Mommy." I told myself, this lady is crazy!!!! She was sure that we were having a girl because she knew what God had told her and showed her.

A few months passed by and my husband and I were planning a small gender-reveal party. Of course, I had to invite her because I wanted to see if she was right all this time. We talked several times on the phone and sometimes I would ask her, Are you sure? She would always say yes.

So, the big day arrived and everyone was waiting and wondering. We were so nervous that day. Deep down inside she knew I wanted a girl so badly. I even told myself that she had better be right. I'm pretty sure she was telling God, "please let me be right because if I'm not, she will kill me." We finally had the note in our hands from the doctor. Everyone's screaming "boy" and she's screaming "girl." I opened the letter, and my husband and I couldn't believe our eyes. The note read, "It's a beautiful girl." We screamed, cried, and laughed all at the same time, but when we looked over, she was looking up telling God, "Thank you."

God revealed to her our blessing, and although we did doubt her vision a few times, she kept her faith knowing what God had shown her. She never lost sight of that and still talks about it to the present day. Our baby is two years old now; she has curly hair and is a beautiful little girl.

Thank you, God, for allowing Lourdes to have the first vision of our big blessing.

Sincerely,
Rafael and Amanda Abreu"

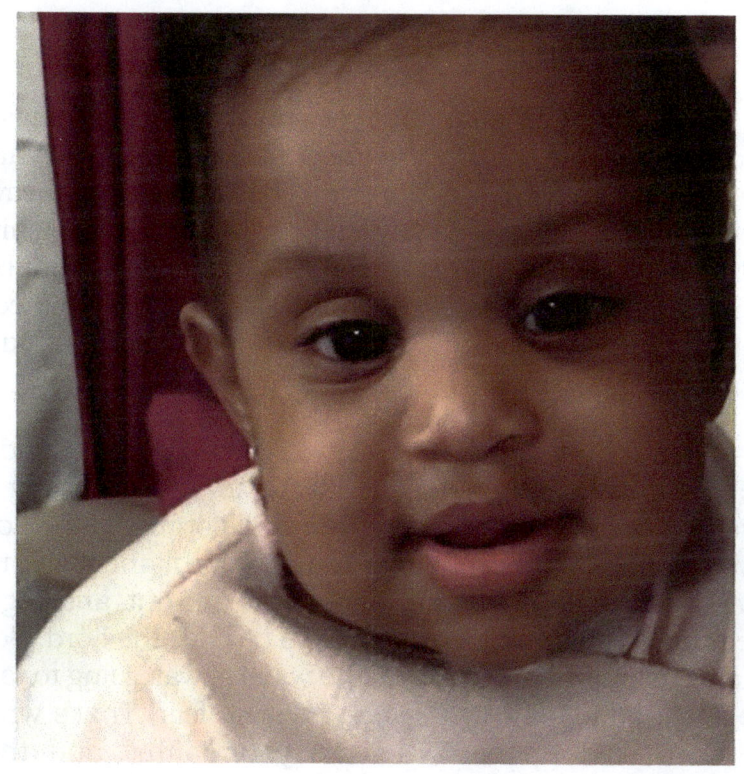

Baby Abreu

Chapter 7

Healed By Faith

I was a new Christian, but very zealous for the things of God. At that time, I had an issue of blood for 21days which the doctors could not seem to stop. The flow was very heavy; and I could not even breathe deeply without it just gushing out. I kept going back and forth to the emergency room but each time, I would be sent back home without remedy. Unfortunately, my blood count began to decrease, making me seriously anemic.

Around that same time, I was invited to a Sunday evening service at another church, in the company of several pastors. As I took a shower and got ready, the Lord gave me specific instructions. Almost simultaneously, the devil began to formulate his plan to take me out, and began speaking to my mind about going to be with the Lord. So, I started asking God if this was the way He was going to take me and I told God I was ready; I felt no fear! That's when the Lord said to me "Where is your faith?" and then instructed me: "lay your hand on your stomach and speak to the issue!" I did! Immediately I could feel it all drying up, but did not fully realize it until I got back home after the service; and realized there was no gush, and no saturation. Amen! I was healed immediately! I just want to assure you that whenever God heals, He heals! We cannot doubt Him; I was almost on that path of doubt.

My pastor had preached at the other church, and when he was finished, he turned the service over to the pastor of the church who hosted the service. The pastor made an altar call for all who have serious health issues and needed a miracle to come forward for prayer – I attempted to get up and suddenly the voice of the Lord echoed in my Spirit "where are you going, you are healed!" Unquestionably when I returned home, there was no flow! It had dried up immediately when God commanded me to take authority. This was on day 21 of the issue. Selah! Let us think about this! On the 21st day of the hemorrhaging, God healed me! Amen. To God be all the Glory!

Chapter 8

The Trance to Africa

A Spiritual Journey

I was praying and fasting one day, and as I laid there in my secret place, I was transported in the spirit to the continent of Africa; specifically, to the regions of Kenya, and Nairobi. In the spirit, I saw Cú, the chief of a defeated tribe, kneeling all alone because his tribe had all been killed and he was being pursued by the victorious tribe. I found myself speaking to him and encouraging him not to be afraid of them.

The sun was very bright, and the ground was parched, and Cú knelt with his spear in his hand stuck in the ground supporting himself. The Lord began to speak to me saying, "inform him that he will become the leader of that tribe who was in pursuit of him." That tribe's leader had been killed, and Cú was afraid, but the Lord assured him that no harm would come to him.

I shared the plan of salvation: that if he would acknowledge Jesus as Lord and Savior he would not have to fight with them because the Lord would fight for him. He knelt and gave reverence to the Lord. Immediately after that he faced the group and began to tell them what Jesus could do for them if they surrendered and dropped their weapons of war. They all sat and listened. Then he arose and led them into the sunset.

The Lord instructed me to sing the song, *Keep your eyes on Jesus*.

> *Keep your eyes on Jesus; keep your mind on Him*
> *Keep your mind on Jesus on that narrow path,*
> *He is in the sunshine, and He is in the rain,*
> *So keep your eyes on Jesus, and He will lead the way.*

I prayed and assured them that Jesus had left His peace with them.

This may seem to be a farfetched story, but I assure you, it is real. There are many supernatural happenings of which we are not aware unless we are sensitive to the Spirit of God and believe that the spirit world actively manifests itself. One truth that I have learned is that there is no distance in the spirit realm; and because of this truth, we can stay in one place and pray for someone or a circumstance in a far distant place, and miracles can and do take place.

We may not always know the outcomes of the journeys of our spirit, but we do know that we are spirit beings and once we submit ourselves to the Father and are willing, He will use us to bring deliverance to someone in crisis. Life with God is an adventure.

I pray that you will have many spiritual adventures with the Holy Spirit.

Chapter 9

Missionary Trip to Mexico

I embarked on a missionary trip to Mexico, specifically to Guadalajara, and Sahuayo. I was excited to reach God's people, and it was a great privilege and honor to serve the Lord in this commission.

He certainly gives us the desires of our hearts. When I was growing up, my desire and confession was, "I want to go to other countries to help people." He heard the confession of my heart and granted my desire.

Another Adventure Begins

We left New York for Guadalajara on December 7th, and were to change planes in Houston, Texas, which we did. After we boarded the plane, the pilot announced that they were experiencing technical difficulties, and inside of me I heard in a loud voice "take me off this plane." Almost simultaneously the pilot announced, "we have to deplane!" I was very happy about that!

A similar incident took place on our arrival in Houston, Texas. After touchdown, the plane taxied for an extensive period of time before it reached the assigned gate. As a result of this delay, we had to rush to make it to our connecting flight. On our way there, we realized that there was a great distance between where we were and where we were going, because the gate to our connecting flight was in another terminal and required us to take an air train. I saw a plane taking off while we were in transit to the gate and jokingly I said to my friends "there goes our plane!" When we finally reached the counter to check in, they informed us that we had just missed our plane connection to Mexico, and we would have to take a night flight or leave the following day. I refused to accept those options.

I explained that we had arrangements in Guadalajara to travel by bus into another town that day. I also informed the agent that it was my first time going there and it was crucial that I get on a flight right away! The favor of the Lord was with us. There was another individual who was ahead of us also waiting for a connecting flight. He was hoping the agent would get him on the plane. The agent stepped away from him for a moment and began searching on another computer and sure enough, she told me that there was a flight leaving in about another hour or so, which I gladly accepted. Another agent came to the counter and asked the man who was waiting if he got a flight and he responded "no." She then asked the agent who assisted me, how did she get a flight for me when there weren't any available. She replied "I don't know" I don't know! It was the favor of God! Hallelujah!! We finally boarded the plane, happy to be on our way. Because of God's favor, we arrived safely in Guadalajara that night and stayed in a hotel overnight because we could not go on the road trip to the other town as planned. The next day we toured the city, visiting a few tourist attractions; for example, the big cathedral.

Later in the evening, we boarded a bus to the City of Sahuayo, where our mission began. On our way to the hotel, our leader was invited to visit a pastor in the town whom she wanted to meet; therefore, we were taken to his church by the very faithful pastor who was our host. When we arrived at the church, they were in bible study.

We introduced ourselves to the group seated around the table. Then the Apostle who was our leader asked me to sing a song that I had sung earlier to another group of people. Here are the words: *Dios ha sido bueno (God has been good)*. Suddenly the Holy Spirit began to prophesy through me saying "Wait on Me! Like in the Upper Room the disciples waited on Me until they were endued with power from on high! Wait for the answer which I will give to you." At this juncture everyone rose to their feet simultaneously worshipping God! The Apostle began to prophesy to the pastor's wife. She told her things that only God knew.

On Sunday we visited their church to worship with them. We enjoyed the worship experience and I also ministered in dance.

Ministering in Dance

Interpreting

Just before the pastor preached, the Spirit of the Lord began to speak through his wife. She began to share with the congregation what took place on Thursday night. She explained to all of us, that they had been seeking God for answers concerning the operation of the gifts of the Holy Spirit, and while seeking, God sent us from afar to bring clarity. She explained that the prophecy was exactly what they were asking and seeking God for.

After the service, in the afternoon, they invited us to eat with them and we accepted. While we were fellowshipping with them, the pastor's wife began to share with us in private that the prophecy which the Apostle shared with her was to the point and other things that lined up with what God had spoken into her heart privately.

Missions Outreach

We visited Palos Altos (tall trees) — a village in a remote area of Jalisco. The road trip was long, but it was worth the drive; lots of open fields for miles. When we arrived at the location, I was moved with compassion like Jesus was *(Matthew 9:36) But when he saw the multitudes, he was moved with compassion on them, because they fainted, and were scattered abroad, as sheep having no shepherd.* The children were playing happily in the dirt with their dogs. Their toys were bottles, sticks, and stones. I saw only one house in the area; their living conditions were not so good, but they were happy and humble. My heart filled up on seeing these people – grown people, youth, and children waiting on us. We sang worship songs and ministered both spiritual and physical food. There was a pregnant teen, to whom we ministered who accepted the Lord as Savior. On another day, we distributed coats and clothes to all the children.

With the children in Los Palos

Visit Another Church Upon a Hill

This church was far away upon a hill. The people were very humble, grateful, and receptive to God's provision. We ministered to the people; there were people with needs that only God through his servants could touch and heal their bodies and mind.

I keep experiencing God's sovereignty — supreme power or authority, and love and concern — for His people. Believe me, when I tell you – He will go to the greatest length to reach His people. The journey was very long, and took us up rocky, narrow roads, between trees, to a remote area where there was nothing. Following the service, on our way back, the car would not go down the rocky hill. We were stuck on the hill with the tires spinning and rocks were flying everywhere, and the car wasn't moving. We exited the car so that the men from the church could attempt to push it off the hill. But no way! In my mind I am thinking it was pitch dark; any animal could have come out at us. Thankfully, it eventually moved. Wow, such sacrifices are made by the many evangelists and missionary workers. The Apostle shared with me beautiful, dangerous missions she has done for the name of Jesus. She would say to me "If you are sold out to Christ, you have to go." Amen to that!

About The Host: Tireless

The pastor who received and hosted us, is a very dedicated man of God. His love and commitment to the work of the Lord and his compassion for God's people are remarkable. He is part of a three-person team. His wife, a young lady he adopted, and himself. They cook for the poor and needy from his resources and income. His tireless sleepless nights have touched my heart. He does not beg for help but uses what he has and maintains his focus on the Great Commission.

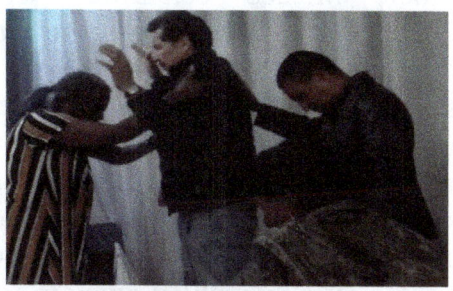

Praying for the saints

Tour of the City of Sahuayo

After all of our missionary work was accomplished, the pastor took us on a few tours on our way back to Guadalajara. We stopped at a really good restaurant up on a hill with a beautiful scenic view. We were able to see the plant where the "Tequila rum" is produced.

Adventure in Guadalajara

God brought us back safely, without incident. It was a long car ride; approximately four hours. We had car problems on our way, so the person who was taking us could not complete the journey. We had to wait until we were able to get a taxi large enough to fit us and our luggage. This new driver was not very familiar with the area where we were headed, and could not find the hotel. When we had circled for a long while I began to get skeptical, but prayerful. I give honor to all missionaries; it is not an easy job, but God always brings us through! That is a testament to the work of the Lord, He is faithful in everything. He promised to preserve us from all evil; to watch our going out and coming in, from this time forth and even forevermore. Upon our return to Guadalajara, we spent a few more days having fun. We visited souvenir shops and marketplace.

A Celebration in the Town

In December, Mexico celebrates the Virgin of Guadalupe. There was a park across the street from our hotel, in which they staged all kinds of colorful performances which we watched and enjoyed. We decided to take a walk and shop some more. While we were walking around, an individual approached me with a great smile and admiration in his eyes. He suddenly reached out and shook my hand so quickly, that I asked myself "what was that all about?" He quickly walked away in the crowd, but kept looking back at me, with a great smile and bright eyes as if he was saying "I have encountered a visitation." I did not know what to make of it; I was puzzled.

Another Mysterious Encounter (Peek-A-Boo)

The following morning, we were (my friend Judy and me) looking for a restaurant for breakfast. We visited one adjacent to the hotel and I entered first because my first language is Spanish. I observed the waiter conversing with some individuals, he was very friendly with them, so I waited for him to acknowledge us, but when I approached him to get a menu or to be seated, he ran to the back of the restaurant leaving us alone.

I waited a few more minutes for him to come out because I thought he had gone to get their order. As I waited, I kept looking back towards the kitchen and to my surprise, he was peeking out from behind the walls like peek-a-boo! It was almost as if he was afraid (or prejudice) because we are people of color. I did not understand his behavior, so we left and found another restaurant. Here I am again not knowing what to think of this encounter. The following day, we returned to the first restaurant, because I had put together a few ministry tracts. I asked for him and they informed me that he was not there. The staff was surprise at his absence because he was not one to miss a day's work. Personally, I don't know if he was on the lookout and had ran to hide again, since I was not being told; therefore, I left the tracts anyway and asked them to make sure he got them. We returned to New York, the following day.

Who Is the Virgin of Guadalupe?

When I returned to New York, I decided to do some research on this Virgin of Guadalupe. I had heard about the celebration of "The Black Virgin" on the news, but did not hear any reference as to her skin color. I *googled* the information, and, as I looked into it, the Lord began to reveal to me that the two mysterious encounters with the two men: (the one on the street in Sahuayo and the other at the restaurant) were similar.

The Black Virgin

The encounter with the gentleman on the street who was so happy was because he thought he had a visitation with the Virgin of Guadalupe, which made him excited. Everyone in that city is Hispanic of a light skin tone, whereas, I am a woman of color. As you probably already guessed, we were the only black people walking around in town.

I give God all the glory! We are spirit beings filled with the Holy Spirit and ambassadors in another country on assignment. This man probably went home and shared with others that he had an encounter. I prayed that the Spirit of God transformed his life and made him a witness and a messenger for the Lord.

In contrast – the individual at the restaurant ran and hid because he was not living right, and was terrified. What we saw on his face was absolute terror! In his mind, he believed the black virgin visited his workplace because he was not right. He certainly ran for his life, because they informed me that he is there every day, but that particular day when I left the literature for him, he did not report for work. Through this incident I learned there is divine protection whether abroad or home. I live in New York and minister locally, every chance I get. God is the revealer of hidden truths and mysteries. Amen.

Chapter 10

Dreams Become Real in Manhattan

Aside from going on ministry trips, I also kept a full-time job. For some time, I had been employed in the Foreign Securities Department at Merrill Lynch, located in the World Financial Center (WFC). On the night before my last day there, I had two dreams. It became apparent to me that my dreams and visions were occurring more frequently. These dreams were very insightful and turned out to be a ghostlike prophecy revealing possible devastation that could impact many.

The First Dream: Water Sputtering

It was a very hot night in 1989, and while in a sound sleep, I dreamt that I was looking out my office window from the WFC. I could see the Westside Highway, the Hudson River, and the World Trade Center (WTC). All the other towers were visible as well. We were busy working, when suddenly, there was tumultuous eruption from the outside, much like a bomb explosion. The building was hit. Water sputtered everywhere.

The Smoke

The fumes quickly filled up the room to the 10-feet ceiling. Still in the dream, I envisioned that my co-workers panicked. They were terrified and ran toward the door and out of the room. Selina, my assistant supervisor was about to rush out with the crowd. In the dream, I forcefully snatched her back and grabbed her hands. Together, we struggled under the tons of water now rising in the room. Instinctively, I knew that not everyone who ran out of the building would survive. Gasping for breath, I urged her not to rush out. We held on to each other tightly. It seemed like an eternity. Struggling for breath underwater was no time for long prayers.

I could only think of the words of the 23rd Psalm, *The Lord is my Shepherd; I shall not want...* Even then I was exasperated. Gripping Selina's hands once again, I continually kept trying to convince her that we had to survive. Even at that moment, my faith was strong. Suddenly the water began to recede. It seemed as if an enormous sponge absorbed all the moisture in the room. Miraculously, we were safe. As is usual in dreams, the scene abruptly changed. [I was in another dream-like state of mind].

I looked out the window overlooking the Hudson, and to my amazement, all the towers had fallen and crumbled. Even the World Financial Center was full of debris. There was destruction everywhere. Even on the inside of the window ledge, there was debris. I was wondering how that was possible, since there was no broken window. This alarmed me even after I woke up; but the dream seemed unusually real. I felt that it would probably nag at me all day. The details just did not match up to anything I knew.

As I shared my dreams at work the next day, my coworkers were eager to hear all the details. We talked about all the possible meanings throughout the morning. As we analyzed the details, it only stirred up more mystery in our minds. However, there is nothing that could have prepared us for what happened in reality, on that same day. There were two bombing incidents! The first bomb had been set near the WFC building. Hearing the emergency alarm, we learned that our building was one of the targets. Target?

Of what? We did not know what to believe. Moving quickly as trained, we hid under tables and desks, preparing for any potentially hazardous debris. Would it be the same as I saw in my dream? We all braced for the worse.

With enormous speed, emergency vehicles and police sirens arrived. Our voices echoed disbelief. We knew it could explode. Over the speakers, we learned that the authorities had discovered a bomb near our building! It was planted in the crosswalk between 165 Broadway and the World Financial Center, where we often walked for lunch. Fortunately, it did not blow up! The New York City (NYPD) Bomb Squad was able to deactivate it in time.

The explosion could have been deafening. Sirens and smoke could have filled up the hallways. We would have been trapped and terrified. Possible terrorist attacks could be happening at our location. I tried to stay calm. Our imagination went wild.

Co-workers' voices screamed out at me! "There goes your dream!" Agitated, I insisted and said, "no it isn't!" They shouted, "why not?" I explained, "The details don't line up" the dream was very specific. Little did we know what would happen later, within weeks.

Another bomb was set. This one exploded under the parking lot, near where we walked daily. It exploded! It happened! Anxiety levels skyrocketed. We all felt even more unsettled, filled with worry and concern. "God Help Us," I prayed. We just wanted to go home. Miraculously, we were soon safe and sound again. We were nervous for a long time after the bombing. I stayed in prayer. Even individuals who never prayed, openly thank God, that no one was hurt. As I thought about what happened, it seemed like a dress rehearsal for worse to come — something, none of us wanted to imagine. While retelling my dream, I adamantly added "that isn't it!". That's not what my dream showed. The bomb incidents just did not match up with the dream. After many days, the bombing incident became a past, foggy memory. We managed our unspoken apprehensions. We hoped the bombing was over.

The Second Dream: Twinkling of an Eye

I dreamt that my supervisor, Mr. Dixson's wife, Jean Marie was pregnant. Her stomach seemed unusually large and, in a flash, or in a twinkling of an eye, she was pushing a baby stroller, and in it was a beautiful baby girl dressed in pink. The Spirit of the Lord spoke to me saying "tell her husband, Mr. Dixson to be appreciative of this girl and love her with all of his heart and I will bless him with the son he desires."

Mr. Dixson's Story

Mr. Dixson shared his story with me. As a young couple they were very excited to start a family together, and subsequently, were blessed with a son. They decided to have a Christening ceremony for him, and it was a memorable time with friends and family. During the celebration the baby fell asleep and they laid the baby in his crib and continued to entertain.

When the celebration was over, they entered the baby's room. To their surprise, they found baby Anthony dead in his crib. Jeanie was overcome with grief. The crib death remained as an extremely sad memory for both of them. Mr. Dixson did not talk very much about their loss, nor the deep level of his hurt and disappointment. Since I viewed myself as an inexperienced Christian, I did not know much about evangelizing, but I tried to be supportive. So, I attended the funeral and I would often reach out to the couple over time. Even on busy workdays, I would take time out to ask about his wife, and to wish her well.

Months passed, until the Word of the Lord came to me saying "Go and tell that young man (Dixson) that I will restore his son because I do not take away and not give back or replace that which I take away" "I need him to release Me," says the Lord; He said the young man is "angry with Me and blames me for the death of his child. He needs to let go of all unforgiveness and I will bless him." I did just what the Lord commanded me to do.

On the day I gave Mr. Dixson that word from God, he looked at me in awe and with some disbelief. I would later learn that, according to the CDC, Sudden Infant Death Syndrome (SIDS), had declined considerably — from 13.3 deaths per 100.00 live births in 1990 to 35.2 deaths per 100, 000 live births in 2018. Regrettably, little Anthony's death may have added to those statistics. Studies show that SIDS has no symptoms or warning signs. In other words, there is nothing the young couple could have done to save the life of their infant child. Babies who die of SIDS seem healthy before being put to bed. Nevertheless, this was no comfort to the young couple.

The couple tried several times to conceive again, but to no avail. They had visited many doctors and the report they received was that they will never have children; so, they gave up trying. I kept reminding him of the Word of the Lord as the years passed by. I realized he was at ease with God. Only the Lord knows the heart of man. He knew exactly when to intervene with His promises. I assured Dixson that God will do just what He said. It was clear that he wanted to believe. It was good enough for me to know that at least he would think about the promise.

Finally, I would have another message to share with Mr. Dixson, who often teased me about my dreams. He would joke and say, "oh, another dream? What did you eat last night?" We would laugh together, until one morning in August, 1989 when I had a confirmation.

It was around 5:00 am when I called Mr. Dixson. I told him that his wife would become pregnant. 'It will be a girl! Love her and then God will send you a son. He jokingly exclaimed "Lord, knows, we are trying." Afterwards, I shared about my previous dream concerning the destruction of the world trade center. He did not take me seriously, but I guaranteed that it would come to pass.

Leaving Merrill Lynch

While at Merrill Lynch, my office had been located in the Foreign Securities Department, housed in the WFC. The official announcement came that my company would soon be relocating to New Jersey. I remembered being told that several co-workers decided not to transfer. Taking the same option meant an unplanned career change. I experienced "bitter/sweet" emotions because I knew that I would miss my co-workers. My supervisor, Mr. Dixson, had been particularly instrumental in my training with the company. He would be transitioning as well. His support to all of us was invaluable. With my experience in a corporate setting, trained by capable professionals like Mr. Dixson, I knew I could easily pursue and qualify for another lucrative position.

I mused that maybe a change was good. In a few days, my change would take place through a call from the United States Postal Service (USPS). I was instantly hired. The hours and salary were competitive. It was like a dream come true.

I could now spend more time with my children, attend Parent Teacher Association (PTA) meetings, volunteer in the community center, and take walks in the park. There were perks working in Manhattan near the WTC. It was blocks away from the National Memorial & Museum, and Manhattan Waterfront, and of course, the Woolworth Building a few streets over where I could catch great buys as surprises for the children. I would occasionally treat myself to chocolates or cuppa from Nunus on the way home.

As I raced to the train at WTC station, I blended in with the crowd with similar speed, oblivious as I rushed to my destination. I walked swiftly to work that last day, with gifts in my hands, turning familiar corners. Daily, as I would push the elevator button, I often marveled at the height of the NYC buildings. For instance, the Empire State Building, concealing an indestructible 60.000 tons of steel, 10 million bricks, 730 tons of aluminum and stainless steel, would always stand tall and proud. I reasoned soundly that the WTC, being taller, was invincible. I felt secure even on the 12th floor at Merrill Lynch with Mr. Dixson, as we all did. As our unit was being broken up, saying our goodbyes was bittersweet.

Bear Hugs in the Office

On the morning of my last day at Merrill Lynch, when Mr. Dixson arrived, he called me into his office and quickly shut the door. At this point I had no idea what was going on; our department dealt with foreign securities and I wondered whether I had made a booking mistake. His office was all glass. The co-workers were in an open space. All eyes were on us. Abruptly, I handed over the gift I had selected for him and his wife, as my way of continuing to encourage; but he quickly laid it aside on the edge of the desk. Tall and bold as he was, he stood up from his chair and gave me a bear hug. By that, I assumed, that at least my job was not in jeopardy.

In a mischievous kind of way, he asked me to repeat the dream, and I did. With his usual wide grin, he flopped down in his chair. He leaned back; crossed and uncrossed his arms. Grinning, he reached for me again. I could see sheer happiness in him as I had seen in my grandfather when I would surprise him on a visit. His contagious laughter was as large as his giant-like hands. I would laugh, even if I didn't know what was so funny. That moment was like that for me. "Ahaaa, Mr. Dixson is just being silly; he's always teasing me about my dreams."

Mr. Dixson gazed at me intently, in the same manner that Pluto and my sister Jeronima would after being drenched from the dock—and I waited. Then, Dixson was up again. Was he going to run? In the office? Did he get the Holy Ghost? I took a quick peek. Yea, all eyes were still gazing through the glass at both of us. In the meantime, I was trying to figure it all out, when suddenly he hugged me, repeatedly. He kept a wide smile. But he was not telling me anything. Exhausted, but seemingly liberated, he finally sat down and began to fervently explain his excitement. Pulling his chair up close to hold himself still, he said, "I have good news."

"My wife, Jeanie went for her annual check-up. The doctor did a routine urine test as part of the visit. She is pregnant! Hallelujah!" My mouth dropped open. I was thrilled beyond words. This was the fulfillment of the dream! He pounded his fist on the desk and jumped straight up again. Clearly, out of character and a bit off-balance, he sat back down. I will never forget how Dixson, repeatedly, whirled himself around in that office chair. Sheer joy took over. I felt like joining him, but I didn't. I was overly excited for them both. It was a bonding moment for me with this lovely couple. On leaving his office, I took the liberty to add: "it will be a beautiful girl! She's coming." We agreed.

After having been childless for five years, they would finally end up with three new blessings. "Remember to thank God. He did what he said he would do. Hallelujah!" we both yelled. We didn't care about being overheard in the office. By now I was considered a psychic of sorts, anyways. I rejected the psychic label.

My dream of the devastation at WTC (World Trade Center) stimulated many office conversations. I have always told my coworkers that I serve a big God who keeps big promises. In the twinkling of an eye, amazing things happen. This, all from an all-knowing divine Father.

It would take some time, but I would soon welcome my new responsibilities. I felt that it was like a dream come true. I focused my attention on a new job, new school year, my children's report cards and enjoying my favorite time of year, Fall. Little did I know another dream would come true all too soon.

A Vision That Would Be Startling

It was now 2001, some years later. I had long left the WFC building; and by now I was secured in my new position at the United States Postal Service (USPS). I excelled in my new job quickly, and was proud of my progress. Revamping my career had been the right move. Change was in the air, and I welcomed the challenge. Often, however, I would reminisce about friends and my old job at the WFC. My previous dreams and visions were forgotten.

The date was Monday, September the 10th when I left work feeling unsettled. My family was waiting for me at home, and the air conditioning there felt good that evening; it was nice to be home. After a quick greeting to the family, I hurried to my room ignoring well-meaning gestures to join in. Sitting on my bed, I felt even more burdened. I just could not shake the dreadful gnawing. It felt like a woman travailing in childbirth.

Tears of sadness overwhelmed me. I began to weep uncontrollably and fell on my knees before God. I could not understand what was wrong, so I interceded. However, even praying fervently brought me little relief.

It had been an unusually warm day in September; and during my intense travail, a vision occurred. A vision usually has more clarity than dreams and reveals much more. Such was the case at this time. I saw a hotel, in the area of Church Street in Manhattan near the World Trade Center. There was a gentleman (a valet) standing under the green awning canopy. Another one was standing in front of the building. Suddenly, there was a couple who were quickly ushered through the front doors. They looked afraid and worried, as they were swiftly pushed into a square-shaped vehicle. As I was thinking of how odd this was, I heard in my spirit "It's a hostage situation." I was alarmed and hoping for a better outcome in real life.

When I had entered the room to pray, it was sunny outside. I prayed for many hours until nightfall. Eventually, it became dark; and, wide awake but still in a vision, I was looking out the window overlooking the Hudson River. I observed the scene across the river, bright lights seem to beam, illuminating the buildings. I closed my eyes to prepare to pray. I was not prepared for what I would see next.

Later in the evening, I was released from the prayer room and I went and had a bite to eat. My friends said to me "Lourdes, we are sure God has granted your petition, based on the intensity of your prayers," they heard me praying the entire time. They were encouraging. Still, I did not feel settled. It was an unshakable burden. It didn't make sense. The details of the vision did not seem connected except the site of the WTC. My night went by. Nothing out of the ordinary occurred. It all seemed like a bad dream; which I hoped it was.

It Was Not a King Kong Movie

My memories of Merrill Lynch are reserved as a good experience. I had finished my training at the post office, and on this particular morning, on turning my calendar, it read Tuesday, September 11, 2001. It was a clear day; but now, looking back, many agree that there was "something" lurking in the atmosphere. Neither the dreams and vision of the scene of crumbled skyscraper buildings over the Hudson, nor the kidnapping scene at the hotel on Church Street in Manhattan near the World Trade Center, prepared me for what would happen that day. Years prior, coworkers had echoed chilling thoughts when a second bomb had exploded; but today, the incredible was about to happen.

I finished my cup of tea and reviewed my agenda. It was morning break, around 9:00 am in New York. Everyone had to be punctual at the USPS, so I hurried to the cafeteria. I overheard muffled chatter about the WTC, then noticed a group of employees intently gazing out of the windows. None of us could comprehend or articulate what was happening. It looked like the remake of yet another King Kong movie, I thought out loud.

A worker standing next to me cursed me in his agony; mouthing unbelievable words, "It's no movie!" My ears went numb. I could only see his big red tongue and scowling teeth.

Turning and looking out the window, I noticed heavy smoke in the air. Without knowledge of what had happened, I thought that the fragments falling from the

WTC windows were pieces of paper. Within seconds, however, my vision cleared. I realized they were bodies of people! People were jumping out of the windows!

I was stunned! The sight was surreal. Realizing the gravity of the scene, someone screamed, "they are jumping out and falling!" The numbers could not be counted. It started a domino effect of hysteria which echoed throughout our building. We all pushed up against each other to see more. I felt small and helpless. We wiped tears and wandered around in a daze. The chilling scene seemed never-ending. What was next? We did not know.

Then the second plane crashed into the side of the building at 9:05 am; the explosion was so great that all we saw was a gigantic ball of fire. Oh my Jesus! I could not grasp the sight; my eyes and mind did not believe what I was seeing. It was the warning in my dream from 1989. Today's date was 9-11-2001. Some of us crawled, we slumped, panicked, and screamed. Still at the window, I was an emotional wreck. My elbow up on my cheeks, with my feet, pressed to the floor. I will not "lose it," I thought, but I did.

Later, we dialed loved ones to let them know our building had not been attacked. It was such a relief to finally speak to our family, but it would be some time before we were all ushered safely out of the building. The authorities warned that we could be attacked next. "Exit the building, exit the building now!" blared over the intercom. Those who could run did so, others were escorted out to safety.

In route, I overheard more bad news. Flight 11 crashed into the North Tower of the World Trade Center and the South Tower of the WTC collapsed. Flight 77 was hijacked, and Flight 175 crashed into the South Tower of the World Trade Center. Unfortunately, Flight 93 was also hijacked.

Even the visions I had could not have prepared me for the horrendous impactful events. One reporter recapped; "Many lives were lost. It's unbelievable." My tears were not held back, thinking of the hijacked planes and those who would not see their loved ones again. It would make a tremendous impact on my heart for many months, even years to come.

Exasperated, I hurriedly walked from 9th Avenue and 33rd Street to 3rd Avenue, to get on the bus uptown. As I got to the corner, the Lord said: "It has been 12 years today and the dream has come to pass." This was an unexpected revelation. I did not fully remember until God impressed that detail in my mind. My reaction was "What dream?" I looked up and noticed I was at the cross streets of 33rd and 3rd Avenue. A particular scripture came to mind as I crossed the street. Jeremiah 33:3: "*Call unto me, and I will answer thee, and show thee great and mighty things, which thou knowest not.*" This was a time for everyone to call on God and I was no exception.

On the bus ride, people were weeping, stunned, and children were bewildered. There was tension, fear, and anguish flooding through conversations, all at once. As I listened, trying to put the pieces together, I arrived at my stop, but mentally, couldn't seem to move. Somehow, my feet stepped into the aisle and guided me. I could still smell the stench of debris. It was the smell of death. We walked on, my feet and I. The comfort of my sofa seemed so far away; but we would make it. I was depending on and calling unto God according to the scriptures. When I finally reached my front stoop, I let out a sigh of relief. We were all well, safe, and on the ground. I hugged myself.

My family covered me with tears and words of thanksgiving. They were well aware of the depressing news reports. In the midst of it, they commented on my travailing prayer the night before. To us, it was related. We were all in awe of the manifestation. They too had to draw on faith—the only source of peace we all had. I did not know at that moment how the pieces would be aligned to the dreams and visions I had in 1989. I relived the scene of people jumping from the WTC throughout that night and many more nights. I did not think I could ever forget the complexity of that day.

Even now, as I pen my story, that day—looking out of the USPS window—remains very real. It is like it was yesterday. Recalling the details still humbles me. Over 2,606 people, who were in the World Trade Center and on the grounds, perished just blocks from my previous place of work.

I believe that the interpretations of my dream and visions were as follows:

The bomb and the water-filled room represented the tons of water used to extinguish the fire and explosives.

Debris on the windowsills: the intrusive fragments of brick and mortar from the burning buildings.

Destruction: human lives that were destroyed in the World Trade Center building, on the grounds, and in planes.

Excessive lightning: blazing fire from the World Trade Center, other buildings, and planes.

Hostages: the trapped hostages aboard the planes.

It was possible that the two bombs near my office building were planted as a test or warning about the forthcoming disaster, which turned out to be the attacks of 911. The memory still clouds my mind and will forever touch the depths of my heart. I am being transparent as I write this book. It is an honest account of what I, and so many others, lived through—still saddened by the heaviness and sight of the loss of lives on 911. This dreadful day impacted the world. What helps me cope is my relationship with my Creator and my faith. I am still so pleased at the omnipotence of my Lord, the all-powerful, all-knowing, and forever-present God remains my daily comfort.

Several years had passed; and while I was secured in my new position at the USPS, I deliberately kept busy, realizing that life would never normalize. I continued to be proud of my progress, excelling in my new responsibilities.

Chapter 11

Ministry on the Night Train

Bale Jr. (not his real name) was my love for several months and I thought it would last forever. He, I thought was my Boaz; my knight in shining amour. It turned out, he was just the opposite. Lack of communication and unfaithfulness started early on; but I stayed in the relationship, even though we were not in agreement as two believers should be.

My efforts to love and be loved continued, but was never appreciated despite my being faithful. Bale did not believe in God the way I did, so devotions and meditations were foreign to him. We grew apart. Because prayers did not seem to be answered, I felt I had disappointed my first love, my God; but there was a part of me that could not let it all go. Feeling guilty, I repented a lot. In the interim, to fill a void and to show my obedience to my heavenly Father, I began to hand out ministry tracts and tell them that Jesus loves them, and that He is coming back soon. I could hear a voice that said, "You are unequally yoked in your relationship with Bale, Jr."

Before I left for work that night He said, "Before the night is over, I will confirm my word to you." 2 Corinthians 6:14 would come to mind: *"Be ye not unequally yoked together with unbelievers: for what fellowship hath righteousness with unrighteousness? And what communion hath light with darkness?"* To me, it was a reminder and promise to take care of me, as I re-aligned myself to His plan for my life—to be a disciple spreading the good news.

Working on the night shift gave me another opportunity to realign my walk with my roots, namely, my belief in Christ. The ministry tracts were not only motivating, they also confirmed the Gospel of Jesus, the Christ. Many of them conveyed the message of salvation, the Resurrection, and end times; so, I would read the Word to the people: "Jesus is Lord. He's coming back to save His people." I was convinced that I was instructed to make this announcement. Night after night I would "bull horn" on the corridors of the train, "Jesus is coming back soon" with my voice. The Lord assured me how much He loved me, and that the scripture would be fulfilled. My Manhattan night ministry gained many followers, and some expected me to bring a 'word" directly from heaven specifically for them. Working for the Kingdom and winning souls was gratifying. I felt God was pleased; and this led me to believe I had the strength to get out and stay out of the toxic relationship. After a while, I no longer craved attention or missed B.J. We had separated for good. A life of peace finally ensued.

Life moves along with ease when we are obedient to His calling. In retrospect, I see how perfectly everything had worked out. I would have this fact divinely confirmed, loud and clear, sometime later. The Holy Spirit was paying attention, even if I was not. No passenger was unapproachable. Besides, it was love that pushed me.

Night after night, arriving on the train platform, my hand would be filled with a new variety of colorful tracts. I began my usual distribution, not even disturbed by those who rejected my generosity. When that happened, I felt that there were other negative forces at hand, and I would say quietly to myself: "That was just Satan!" However, some reactions made me a little nervous and even intimidated, but I knew that God was with me!

While riding the trains, there always seemed to be a seat saved for me. On this particular night, as we were quickly approaching the stop at which I needed to transfer, I stood up and grabbed the pole. No time to do any handouts, I thought. Suddenly, I heard the voice of the Lord distinctly demanding, "Are you going to disobey and not distribute the tracts?" To which I responded, "Lord please help me; give me the courage to do it" and suddenly I felt as if gigantic wings were attached to my back and an increased strength overtook me and I began to distribute the tracts from one end of the transport car to the other.

A genuine hello is a great door opener. I spoke up: "Jesus loves you and He is coming back soon!" Still on the train, and turning to my left, I repeated the words, but this time in Spanish. Simultaneously, a passenger's husband exclaimed with a loud voice, "Gloria à Dios!" (Glory to God). He became the midnight minister. "Lift your hands towards heaven," he said. I knew that kind of authoritative voice. My bags on the seat, we were quite the scene.

"God is confirming His word to you tonight!" He said to me. "That relationship you are involved in, you must leave it alone, because God will bless you!" He confirmed. This mighty man of God, on the train headed to 34th Street Penn Station in Manhattan, had "read my mail!!!" Now, with all my personal life out in the open, it was over for sure! I thought to myself. No more emotional baggage or attachment to B. J. Praise God!

Needless to say, I was in awe of God! If you remember at the beginning of the story, He promised to confirm His word to me before the night ended, and it happened.

This mighty Latino man was bold and reassuring. I was pleased, as God continued to tell me that he had observed and appreciated my persistence. So I continued to reach out, distribute, and encourage people on my train ride, sometimes even missing my own stop. To tell you the truth, my focus was on helping others and touching their heart with something to read. Ministry tracts were helpful miniature pieces of paper. Some with cartoons and others with drawings and scriptures on them. Simply, a handy way to say, "I Love You" or have a good day.

Dating

Bale and I continued to work at the same location, and unfortunately for me, I had to pass by his workstation on the way to mine. One morning, as I walked by his station, curiosity began to get the best of me, and I thought of stopping by to talk to him when suddenly the Lord spoke to me: "Are you going to disobey my orders?' "Do not be unequally yoked." The voice of the Lord was so strong, trust me, I quickly walked away from his area and later resigned from my position, because I did not want to risk disobeying God. After that incident, there was no longer any desire to be with Bale anymore. I often convey in my teaching, the importance of obeying God. He knows what's best. Being unequally yoked with someone who does not have the same belief and mindset as you, can become very stressful. You will always have discord and disagreements. Even in good relationships, there are times when we have disagreements. The Bible in the Book of Amos 3:3 says: *"Can two walk together, except they agree?"* In intimate relationships, there *must* be agreement. Otherwise, the relationship will be overrun with conflict.

Bible Study on the Train

It was a Friday evening, and this particular train ride marked the beginning of some truly exhilarating new adventures. For over a year, I prayed with the usual group for newcomers on our journey. I recall one day traveling from the Bronx on my way to Manhattan, and as I ministered and started distributing bibles; to my amazement, every person opened their bibles and began to read out loud with me. It was like a scene in a church. After I ministered, I would call for anyone who desired to make Jesus their Lord and Savior, and believe it or not, people lifted their hands as I instructed them. I prayed for each one right there and then. Serving God is an amazing life-changing blessing. You would not imagine how hungry people were for the Word of God during their day. There were so many stories of God's blessings on the people, but here I have shared just a few.

A Gift Bag For A Nurse

It was Christmas morning, and I was on my usual route, hoping to find someone to encourage. Initially, when I entered the train, a man sat across from me. He seemed unhappy. I had prepared some packed gift bags which contained socks, scarves, bibles, and goodies. When I entered the train, I would soon acknowledge those close by, and began to minister about God's love. After all, we were approaching a new year, and it was a good time to reflect on how God had brought us all through the previous year. As I proceeded to give out my gift bags to the people who were receptive, I noticed some were speechless. I would later have to transfer to continue my trip, so I watched the time and kept a keen ear open for my stop. Giving gifts was so much fun, that my focus was obscured.

When I sat back down there was one gift bag left over. The Lord instructed me to give it to the man who still looked despondent. I realized that one never knows what frame of mind a person may have. So, stepping towards him, I said hello, handing him my last bag. I told him "God loves you" and I wished him a Merry Christmas. It was a simple gesture of kindness. He eagerly accepted my offer and began to talk openly to me. He had many hurts and disappointments. He went on to explain that he was on his way to work and that he was a nurse at a nearby hospital. He shared that he was recovering from a serious surgery. Having gone through so much in the past few months, he felt a lot of sadness and loneliness, even though he had a good relationship with his girlfriend and a great career.

However, he went on to say that it is the holidays and no one had given him a gift. He felt that he had not even heard "Merry Christmas" from any family members, not even his mother. Unexpected tears poured from his eyes. He carefully wiped them away. I assured him that God loved him. He agreed with me and that God sent a perfect stranger (me) to bless him with a simple gift.

Making my exit toward my continued commute, I reminisced that no one knows what a person is going through (not even a professional in the medical field) until we encounter them close up, God knows all things and always sends His disciples with a message.

Tears Behind Sunglasses

Each time I go out, the Lord will tell me what topic to talk about. I often do not prepare a message from home, because the Holy Spirit guides me. He knows what is needed at that time.

Here I was, ministering on unfaithful relationships, and realizing that the very persons you need to trust are oftentimes the ones who will betray you. In the middle of the message, a lady stood up weeping very hard and she came over and asked me to pray for her. She embraced me for about five minutes, and she wept so uncontrollably that my back was soaked with her tears. Her story was that she just happened to return home after waiting on the train platform because she forgot something and to her surprise, she found her husband in bed with her cousin. She was so devastated, that when she heard the message, she was broken up because it applied to her. She pointed out the reason why she wore these unusually wide sunglasses was to cover her eyes so that no one would see her cry. I assured her that God knows her pain and that He will deliver her from it. Our God is merciful.

A Dirty New Years' Eve Hug

With shivering hands, he lifted the stained coffee cup carefully to his parched lips. I stepped on to the train with a loud greeting: "Good morning, ladies and gentlemen! Oh, I didn't mean to startle you. Please, no need to get up." I kept a pleasant, non-threatening tone. I stood in front of him and said, "Bet that coffee taste good." He nodded nonchalantly, still looking at the floor, bouncing with the rhythm of the rails. I sensed that others were keenly listening to me, the talker, on our otherwise quiet morning commute. Even he was probably a little embarrassed. We both tried to ignore the disapproving stares of the onlookers. I couldn't help but notice that his face looked wizened, dry and wrinkled, almost fossilized. He must have been only in his 50s, I imagined. Living in the extreme cold, no doubt he was warming up on the train. Shivering from hypothermia, he tried warming one hand in his torn pocket. The opening and closing of the train door didn't help. How sad, to be cold and homeless on New Year's Eve.

I was aware that not only hands but feet and even ears can be highly affected in extremely cold temperatures. The man wore a green skull cap, faded, loose khakis, a dark hanging shirt and used army boots; and I couldn't believe it, no earmuffs. For the moment, he was somewhat protected; but his hands needed gloves. He stayed alert, sitting on the edge of the seat watching for security personnel in case he might have to exit the train. None of the on-lookers could piece together why every other day, he would be on board, waiting for a handout; but there he was, without explanation of his eccentric behavior. It was clear that he was non-conforming. He did not want to be like the rest of us. Instead, his rushing in and off the train was predestined. I stayed quiet for a while, thinking and reminding myself to be grateful. Suddenly, my long johns, cotton, (but girly), carefully hidden, felt warmer. I just knew this stranger didn't have on any. Umm, Lord, have mercy!

Intentionally homeless, was beyond my comprehension. The wide-eyed gazes from others confirmed my thoughts; but I was on a mission. Onward to salvation! Let them look. To counter the stares, I looked back at them.

I raised my voice a little higher and said: "You know, Jesus loves you." There I was, on the train again, determined to be a voice in "the wilderness" as I ministered. I decided to talk softly to the homeless man, when the Lord said to give him some money, maybe for gloves, I hoped. I always keep a dollar or some change in the outside pocket of my handbag; but I pulled out a $20.00 bill and handed it to him. He closed his hand quickly without looking at it. "You know God loves and cares for you," I said. His head still bowed, he slowly opened his frostbitten hands and asked softly, "all this for me?" "Yes! It is all for you." He said he had never received such a sum of money from anyone before; and added; "I will always cherish this moment." Finally looking up, he told me his name. At that moment I was filled with supernatural compassion and awe, and praising God, I felt impressed to hug him, green skull hat and all — but I hesitated. It was not my habit to hug strangers — that would take a truly divine intervention. It was an uncomfortable thought, so I didn't think anymore. I would soon be at my stop anyway.

Would you believe that suddenly he asked, "May I hug you?" Wow, by now eyes of everyone were on us. I responded, "sure," and as I hugged back, the audience on the morning train applauded in unison. One passenger who had watched suspiciously all that time, now hollered way from the other end of the aisle, "that's God!" "That's Love!" Wow! Jesus is here! Some of the crowd standing, some leaving, was emotional and ecstatic, still clapping their hands.

Before I exited the train, the passenger at the end of the car was overwhelmed with the display of the love and compassion of Jesus, and began to confess his faults to me. He said he was a backslider and wanted me to pray for him to return to Jesus. I did, and he became emotional, shedding tears. Only God!

The Holy Spirit had warmed and joined our hearts, despite our different paths (mine and Orlando's). This reminded me of one more biblical teaching. According to Matthew 9:36, When Jesus saw the crowds, he felt compassion for them, because they were distressed and dejected, like sheep without a shepherd. God is concerned about people. It is not His desire that any should perish, but that all should come to repentance. Many more opportunities to be guided by God's great love would soon come my way. I would travel a path to the West Indies and to Europe where my heart's desires would come true. The new opportunity would lead me to get reacquainted with previous ministry partners.

Chapter 12

My Path to Europe: Netherlands

I had met my friend Jacqueline several years before in Jamaica, and therefore, I was excited to see her again on arriving in the Netherlands. It would be my first time traveling to Europe, and I knew that we would enjoy our time together. Boarding the second plane, I took a window seat — I love the window seat because it afforded me the opportunity to look out into the skies. I was in full anticipation of what mighty miracles God would do.

We planned to attend a big "Holy Ghost" Conference together, but soon found out that it was canceled. Not to be deterred, she asked me to teach bible study with a group of local church people. I was prepared.

Prompted by the Holy Spirit while in New York, I had selected three sermon outlines and I brought one of them with me to the meeting. No one had seen them previously. When I arrived at the church, Jacqueline introduced me, and we shook hands with the pastor. He had just returned from his trip to Africa, so he decided to sit with his members. I was excited to bring the message. I prayed, and began my topic on Spiritual Gifts from my outline. I taught what God had imparted to me with fervor. I was unaware that this topic was connected to a previous teaching done by the pastor. I continued deep into my message.

At a certain point I noticed that the people were looking at each other with puzzled expressions. I quickly studied their faces. They seemed uncomfortable and in disbelief. I was careful to give scripture references to corroborate my message. I continued for a while longer, and then headed off the stage.

Without knowing why the audience seemed disturbed, I joined Jacqueline on the pew. Finally, the church service ended, and shortly afterward, we were to learn from an individual what the disturbance and seemingly suspicious nature of the people meant. We were informed that where I began my message, was exactly where the pastor had left off. This explained the puzzled looks on the faces of the people. I reassured them that I had not been in his previous meeting, nor had I been in contact with other members of the church. Soon the pastor himself would approach me with the same accusation and suspicious nature, much to my surprise and disappointment.

My Heart Was Sadden

He believed that I had stolen his message. He questioned how I had known to teach on the subject of Spiritual Gifts. How? I could only think, "the Holy Ghost." Unfortunately, the pastor and the members thought that someone had previously told me what to speak about that day. Somehow, they (Believers), did not seem to comprehend that God inspired me, a stranger, before arriving in the Netherlands. Regardless of my insistence, the pastor found it difficult to accept my response. His outspoken words of doubt brought to my mind a sense of his insecurity. His actions were embarrassing and shameful. It was very disappointing and sad to see him act in that manner. At that moment, it did not seem that we were in one accord, serving the same loving God. Scripture-based teaching, prophecy, and words of knowledge, spoken even by a Godly woman, was too much for those "Christians" to receive. I was comforted knowing that it was the Holy Spirit who had prepared me and sent me there from New York. I had brought a timely message to share with the Body of Christ. I would later learn that the church was already under a lot of scrutiny and undergoing discord. Consequently, the people had difficulty trusting anyone — even those among them. Jacqueline and I looked at each other, we knew that it was time to leave. Needless to say, we never returned to that church.

I wished the pastor and his flock well, and moved on, taking my outlines with me. My thinking was, "God is God all by Himself," "no need to steal a sermon." I knew that I was divinely guided and this comforted me. I had spoken up in my defense in an orderly fashion; but I did learn a valuable lesson.

When God speaks to you and gives you a word or a message, you should never doubt. Do not be intimidated. Share it; even if no one believes you. The One who sent you believes in you.

For the next few days during my stay, Jacqueline and I visited the homes of friends. Thankfully, they received my ministry without question. There was liberty, and an awesome flow of the Spirit of God. Thinking back on the pastor's irrational attitude and the reaction of his sheep, I continue to pray for their maturity. It would remain an unforgettable lesson, that would equip me for similar challenges and rejections in the ministry.

Binding Up the Wounded

That first trip to the Netherlands was in 1998; now years later, my friend extended another invitation to my pastors and me. My friend pastors a church in the Netherlands, and she asked us to participate in a conference she had planned. During the weekday we shared the Word of God and many individuals were encouraged.

I had prepared a worship dance to present during the Sunday service. The song was unique and uplifting, and sent a message throughout the whole room. There was special ministry to one person in particular—someone whom God saw as beautiful.

I had a fresh rose concealed in my hands and as I danced the Lord instructed me to call out a young lady whom I did not know previously. As she stepped out into the middle of the room, the Lord said "Tell her that this song is dedicated to her." I did just that, and I began to dance with the rose in my closed hands. At the end of the presentation, I opened my hands and presented the rose to her. Her face lit up and the saints exclaimed in awe! I did not know what it was all about, but then the pastor explained that the young lady's name was Rose! Wow! At this time in her life, she needed encouragement. The saints began worshipping God and acknowledging His amazing act of love towards her. Only God knows what our needs are.

I tell you the truth, my heart was glad to know that God is such a creative and inspiring God. No matter how far you are, God will always send help. I felt as if I accomplished a great task for the Lord because He is so concerned about souls; He moves with compassion when He sees someone in need. He is tender-hearted and always ready to bind up the wounds of the people and heal broken hearts.

God Granted the Desire of My Heart

The desire to fly first class was always in my heart. Before I had traveled to Europe, I always thought that one day I would fly first class to my country, Panama. I thought that would be great—until my trip to Europe! My pastors gave me the dream of my life, by flying me first class! May the Lord continue to bless them and may they continue to experience the favor of the Lord in their lives. This is what I called traveling in style! Let me describe it

I travelled by jumbo jet, in the first-class section. This was not like traveling to Panama where the first-class section was blocked off by a little curtain. Each person had a cubicle with a TV screen; the seat reclined down like a bed. We could get a good night's sleep. The flight was about 8 hours.

The stewardess brought us the newspaper of our choice, and the pastors and I were given the menu. When we were served the appetizer, she graciously waited to remove the utensils and bring the main course. We received hot towels to clean our hands. We were served well.

The full package included a care kit that contained slippers, pajamas, and all the necessary things we needed. The pastor's kindness to me was a reminder that God sends people in our lives to bless us and to reveal the manifestation of His promises. This experience was a demonstration of His unconditional love infiltrating our lives. Only the God I serve would know how to fulfill my heart's desires. So much more joy would come to validate God's plan for my life.

My Ordination

Shortly after my return from my trip to Mexico, the Lord blessed me and established me in ministry. I was ordained. The ceremony was unforgettable. All the rejections of the past did not matter that day.

My ordination was proof of God's true word to me: "*He who calls you believes in you*" despite the fact that there are times in our lives that people will not accept us for who God says we are.

Up to that time, I had experienced rejection on many levels, not only in my personal life but also in my role as an outreach minister and Evangelist. Rejections can cause a delay in progress, but, for me, hope and validation showed up in two extraordinary, anointed vessels.

I now call them my pastors—Apostle Dr. Roberto H. Robinson Sr. and Dr. Monica Robinson. They are well-respected leaders in the Body of Christ. They welcomed me with open arms when I would come to visit before I became a member of the church. Apostle prophesied to me saying "You are coming out" meaning it was my time. I eventually decided to become a member of the Restoration Church of JCA. As is traditional, I was given the right hand of fellowship. I was accepted, not only by the pastors, but by the congregation as whom God says I am. It opened many healing ministry opportunities for me. After the ceremony, I felt settled and content. More evangelizing could be done, being officially ordained and licensed. I was built up and encouraged by the Word of God that was preached. I often thank God for my pastors and their belief in me and their obedience and faithfulness.

Chapter 13

Missionary Trip to Trinidad & Tobago

I was invited to travel to the twin islands of Trinidad and Tobago with a popular missionary team, and I accepted. Our time in Trinidad was another beautiful adventure with God's people. While there we would visit many exotic places.

We ministered in several churches under the leadership of Apostle Mason, the founder of Global Harvest International Ministries. She is known for operating in the demonstration of the miracle gifts of the Holy Spirit.

We also visited a well-respected sister in the Lord. She invited many people who came out to our services. Each one of us ministered a word of exhortation to the people. We also distributed tracts in various cities.

We enjoyed many fun times. We visited the Pitch Lake to which they refer as the 8th wonder of the world and which attracts many tourists. It is said that the waters of the lake have healing properties, and many people take a dip in them to relieve aches. We also toured the shopping area, and took a ride to a hill from where we got a picturesque view of the whole island.

On another day we took the ferry to Tobago, a beautiful country, surrounded by the crystal-clear water of the Caribbean Sea. Part of the experience in Tobago was a place in the middle of the sea called "The Nylon Pool." We traveled by boat to a location about 45 minutes away from the shore, and then, in the middle of the sea, the boat would anchor, and you would disembark into the clear water. The Nylon Pool is a coral pool and the water is about waist deep. I took advantage of this wonderful experience to exfoliate and soak in the warm water. After some time, the tide rose and the water reached up to my neck. I continued to enjoy myself, splashing the water over my head. It was a unique experience.

Chapter 14

Ministry Trip to the Virgin Islands

Police Officer and The Deep Blue

I have always been attracted to beautiful blue sea water; therefore, I took a vacation to St. John and St. Thomas in the Virgin Islands. I had a very good friend whose family lived there, so he allowed me to visit and stay with them. They were very hospitable; it was a blessing. It was a fun trip, and his sister, who is a police officer, took me on a great tour and to the beach. I could not help but admire her focus and commitment to serve the people of the Virgin Islands. As we rode along, she talked about the dangers of the job, but said that it was her life's dream. She spoke of her role to protect the citizens, as intensely as I did about ministering, and she promised that next time we would put our feet into the deep blue water together. She did not stay because she was on duty, so she let me out of the car and waved goodbye. I threw my new straw bag and shades on the soft, colorful terry cloth blanket and sat in the sun.

I kicked off my sandals, and the grainy white sand tickled the bottom of my feet as I stepped into the blue water. I could not resist squatting and soaking my clothes. It felt good, I could breathe effortlessly. Asthma attacks were forever gone. God had healed me so long ago. I felt free. Being in the ocean in the Virgin Islands felt almost as refreshing as diving off the pier with my sister, Jeronima, back in Panama. Oh! to have those childhood days again; skipping, and running around in the sun. At that moment, I embraced the good memories of home.

God had opened that door of opportunity for me to enjoy the pleasure of being there, but being children of God often means we are never off duty; because as ambassadors for Christ, we must always be ready to serve. This would prove true, at a church meeting later that night.

I accompanied my friend's mother to her church and while there, was asked to pray for the sick. Many came believing and were instantly healed. But much to my regret, her mother fell ill and became unconscious. Everyone was alarmed. We all began to pray and went into deep intercession for her soul and her life. Much to our relief, she woke up! Praise our Lord! We shouted! It was only God's power that infused her with life and revived her. Praise the Lord for the great things He has done!

Chapter 15

There Is No Distance in The Spirit Realm

Prayer for a Man in London

I frequently get together with other believers to address various prayer requests and to intercede for those in need. On this particular day as we prayed, my friend, Gayle, received a call requesting prayer for a family member who resides in London. The young man, Lamonte, was paralyzed from his neck to his toes (quadriplegic) and had been bedridden for some time, but I knew that nothing is impossible with God.

Gayle asked me to lead the intercession, and she stood in agreement with me. At that moment, I felt virtue leaving my hands, and I stretched them out as a point of contact. I was able to relate to the experience of Jesus when He felt virtue (power) leaving His body and flowing into the woman with the issue of blood.

According to Luke 8:43-47: A woman in the crowd had suffered for twelve years with constant bleeding, and she could find no cure. She touched the fringe of his robe. Immediately, the bleeding stopped. "Who touched me?" Jesus asked. Everyone denied it, and Peter said, "Master, this whole crowd is pressing up against you." You see, it could have been anyone. "Someone deliberately touched me, for I felt healing power go out from me." When the woman realized that she could not stay hidden, she began to tremble and fell to her knees in front of him. The whole crowd heard her explain why she had touched him and that she had been immediately healed (NLT).

The young man in London was not previously ill; he was strong and going about his daily business; but suddenly became paralyzed — not being able to comb his hair, brush his teeth or feed himself. When I felt the virtue (power) flowing from my fingers, I guaranteed my friend the miracle had occurred. I knew what Jesus meant when He said in the scripture above "I felt healing power go out from me."

From that time on, whenever I prayed and sensed power leaving me, the prayer warriors knew what had taken place. They knew that healing took place. Even if I do not sense it, I know by faith that God has intervened. We Christians walk by faith and not by sight. Without unwavering faith, it is impossible to please God. It does not matter how far a person is geographically, God can reach him in the spirit realm instantaneously. God is omniscient (all-knowing), omnipotent (all-powerful), and omnipresent (present everywhere at the same time). Realizing this truth, all credit is due to the Father. Therefore, I take no glory for the work the Lord does through me. All believers are vessels. Our Lord is the One who heals, makes the deaf to hear, the lame to walk and the blind to see.

Later, that very evening we got the praise report that Lamonte suddenly got up out of the bed and began to brush his teeth and take care of himself. It was a happy report. Glory to God! He is the healing Balm in Gilead and London, and so many other towns and cities.

Chapter 16

Ministry Trip to Nicaragua

Lost Siblings in Nicaragua Found: Hallelujah!

My father was born in the City and Port of Bluefields, which is the capital of the South Caribbean Autonomous Region in Nicaragua. Nicaragua is a Central American nation set between the Pacific Ocean and the Caribbean Sea. It is known for its vast terrain of lakes, volcanoes, and inviting beaches. The scenic views are breathtaking, and was almost as exhilarating as my visit with my siblings whom I had never met. It was the homeland of my father and his two sons, my blood brothers. My father had been friends with their mother long before we were born, but rarely talked about his other children. Therefore, the idea of having other siblings aside from my immediate family was very foreign to us. Our Nicaraguan family connections were mysterious, but I was determined to make contact.

My sister and I, the younger ones, always knew we had each other, and Pluto, of course. Besides that, Mommy and Dad seemed to laugh a lot together. Surely, that was love.

Our Dad was nowhere near perfect, but we were too young to know that then. The drunkenness and loud arguing often crusted in my ears. It was frightening then — and even now, as I think back. The bad memories still linger. The truth is, it was a broken home. My mother tried to protect us as much as she could, but would one day, not be able to do so. She, like so many of her neighbors and cousins, was a victim of domestic abuse. She too, like many of the women in the community, was once young and very beautiful with a desire in her heart to love and be loved. Dad would steal her dream away with his rage. As children we learned to ignore the horrible beatings that would eventually cause serious injury to my mother. Sadly, she never fully recovered. Even worse, my father never apologized for any of his wrongdoings. My mind would often question the incidents that so often occurred on those days and nights, filled with chaos.

How many women go through, not only the pain of abuse, but shame and self-blame? This is even true in the church among many Christians, especially pastors' wives. I knew from experiences, that even boys and girls were often abused in the pews of the church. As missionaries, we were not only prayer warriors, but were often in a war zone, fighting for survivors. Consequently, I made it my mission to study the topic.

According to the World Health Organization's (WHO) latest report, published by PAHO/WHO in collaboration with the US Centers for Disease Control and Prevention, in 12 Latin American and Caribbean countries studied, between 17% and 53% of women interviewed reported having suffered physical or sexual violence by an intimate partner. Back home, had it not been for my grandparents, life could have been more traumatic. It took the whole village to raise two adventurous baby girls.

As I pre-packed for my trip to Nicaragua, I would continue to feel my mother's pain. I did not know whether my healing would come from knowing much more about my father's sons and their lives; but at least that was my hope, as I reached out. I had picked up the phone book, found a familiar family name in the Nicaraguan directory, and dialed a number. As it turned out, the person who answered was another close relative named Jeremiah. He answered the phone cheerfully and confirmed that he knew my brothers well. As we spoke, he introduced himself as a local pastor; Hallelujah! Needless to say, we both had many questions, and during our lengthy conversation, we shared a lot of confirming information and decided to exchange more details and photos.

I conferred with my sister and we eagerly decided to embark on this journey together. We would travel to Nicaragua by faith, realizing that many years had passed, and my father was now deceased. He could not cause any more harm, but he also could not provide any answers. I knew that his sons would be in their 60's at the time of my search; and secretly, wondered if we would ever meet them. Somehow, I knew, the time was right and that it was imperative that we connect in person. My efforts to locate them would be a huge walk of faith and of trusting my instincts. We were two girls, our father's daughters seeking to find missing pieces of ourselves and our lost siblings.

I traveled from New York to Panama to meet her and then we boarded a plane to Nicaragua. Sitting in silence as we landed, we secretly knew that nothing was impossible with God. We hoped together. When we arrived, the pastor was waiting to greet us, and he embraced us both. It had been a long flight. The pastor was delightful and full of enthusiasm. We gathered our luggage, and were finally on our way to get acquainted with our blood brothers. Pastor Jeremiah sat with his driver (who was more of a tour guide) as we made chit chat. He casually invited us to make a quick stop at his home on the way. We excitedly agreed.

What a Pleasant Surprise!

The pastor kept our quest and visit a top secret. We were ecstatic upon our arrival at his lovely home; because, unbeknownst to us, he had invited our brothers for dinner.

We greeted them frantically—face to face for the first time! All of my apprehensions melted as they embraced us in their strong arms; laughing and kissing them both. They later admitted having some skepticism as well. Can you blame them? However, that soon passed. After sharing many colorful stories of our family history, it was clear that we were our father's children. It was such a comfort to finally have brothers. They genuinely expressed the same feeling towards us. They looked at us intently and with amazement and tenderness as if we were porcelain dolls. Mission accomplished! We ate beans and rice and so many new foods until we were full. The long-awaited encounter was glorious.

My brothers in Nicaragua

We all had stepped out in faith. Fear of the unknown was forever gone. For me, this was not only a ministry trip, but it was also putting the pieces of my emotional life together. The void of not knowing my father's children would now forever be filled. Childhood pain was mended in this never-before-shared space with my new brothers. Love, straight from Heaven, unfolded and embraced me. It was the healing I had longed for for many years.

Evangelization

In my travels over the years, I have earned many sky miles, as well as countless souls for the kingdom. I have practiced the following personal principle: when the plane touches down in a country, I claim the land and its inhabitants for the Lord! Therefore, when I set foot on Nicaraguan soil, I also claimed it! In this case, as in every ministry trip, I claim and saw victories after victories.

I came ready and equipped with gospel literature for distribution, as I would normally do on my daily commute to and from work. The day after our arrival we went out into the town where the people were hungry for God.

Even when the adversary tries to steal from me, I count it joy, because God always intervenes. Here is an example. While in Nicaragua, I was standing at a street corner with some tracts in hand and suddenly a man rushed up and snatched one out of my hand and ran away. This amused me, because it gives me so much pleasure to reach people for the Kingdom of God. Evangelism is God's greatest desire.

The Bible states in 2 Peter 3:9 "The Lord is not slack concerning his promise, as some men count slackness; but is longsuffering toward us, not willing that any should perish, but that all should come to repentance."

Before I continue with my story, I extend this invitation to you: If you do not know Jesus as your personal Savior, Deliverer, Healer, and friend, you can embrace this once-in-a-lifetime opportunity to do so by simply following these steps. Please read and verbally confess the following... According to Romans 10:8-11 (AMP), *"Dear Lord Jesus, I repent of my sin and turn from my wicked way, and I accept you as my Lord and Savior. Come into my heart today. Thank you, God."* It's that easy. Congratulations!

In other words, you just acknowledged and confessed with your lips that Jesus is Lord. You believe that God raised Him from the dead, and now, you are saved! Study the Word of God and help evangelize the world. Start as I did, share the Gospel with your spouse, coworker, neighbors, and children.

For with the heart a person believes (adheres to, trusts in, and relies on Christ) and so is justified (declared righteous, acceptable to God) and with the mouth, he confesses (declares openly and speaks out freely his faith) and confirms [his] salvation (AMP).

The Scriptures go on to say,

No man who believes in Him (who adheres to, relies on, and trusts in Him) will (ever) be put to shame or be disappointed.

But what does it say? The Word (God's message in Christ) is near you, on your lips and in your heart; that is, the Word (the message, the basis, and object) of faith which we preached (AMP).

The Local Church with My Sister: Our Last Stop

While in Nicaragua, Jeronima and I were invited by my brother to the local church. We ministered the written Word of God, and also worshipped in praise dance. Additionally, we prayed for many, especially for the sick.

Even today, we firmly believe in God's purpose and plan, that is, to do His perfect will. The Holy Spirit continues to guide us daily with incredible adventures. As a result of years of mission trips together, many people stayed in touch with us both from the pastor's spirit-filled congregation, as well as neighbors. Night after night, during our visit with my brothers, the neighbors would assemble themselves at my nephew's house. In our first service, there were only a few people present, but the numbers quickly grew. Later, when we returned home to the United States, my nephew was kind enough to help us stay in touch using social media. Therefore, because of the contacts we made, we are able (along with the help and support of other churches) to be a source of supplies and other resources for them.

I often think about my travels to Nicaragua as part of a mission around the world. The Nicaraguan cuisine, simple and straightforward, was so appetizing. I can still taste the delicious Gallo Pinto dish, a favorite among the local folk. My family, like me, seemed to enjoy the fresh tropical juices that are so popular there. I was so thrilled to share my journey with my sister Jeronima, we still revel with joy at the opportunity to have had finally met our brothers, my father's sons — men now with families of their own.

When we traveled as groups, the saints would say they were thankful for the kindness of the people as well. There are vivid memories of families arriving by car, planes, sometimes from far-away farms, or even by boat. Still, others walked for miles. It was often a hardship for many, but, arriving and experiencing the presence of God, they felt the trip was worth it. In Nicaragua, there are two seasons, the rainy season, and the dry season. Typically the weather never stopped church services.

At many of these services, hundreds of new church folks accepted Jesus as their personal Lord and Savior. These dear people would take what they learned, the Gospel of Christ, back home to share with their communities. They reported that many meetings continued. After we left, countless individuals came to know Jesus and their lives changed. Marriages were restored, children were equipped to attend college, and businesses prospered. We were fortunate to find so much favor with well-trained local pastors and congregations in the cities where we visited.

Even though I am back in Manhattan, my outreach ministry still continues today to the people in my father's homeland, Bluefields. Bibles, ministry tapes, daily devotionals, and gifts are received with grateful hearts. Pastor Jeremiah is still doing awesome work in his church. I can't help but think that God is so pleased with him. I receive words of thanks from the people of Nicaragua with whom my father's family has shared the Gospel. From my heart, I thank them more.

I am convinced that there is no distance in the spirit realm, and that has been my experience. I have seen the lame walk and the dead raised. The missionary trips to Africa, Mexico, The Netherlands, Trinidad and Tobago, The Virgin Islands, and meeting special friends in Nicaragua have made an indelible imprint on my life.

My comfort when I minister is that I am in the perfect will of God, guided by the Holy Spirit, whether it is ministering at work or abroad. The Holy Spirit is referred to as the Lord and the Giver of Life in the Nicene Creed. He is also called The Creator Spirit, present before the creation of the universe and through His power, everything was made in Jesus Christ, by God our Father. The reference I like best is found in John 14:26, which states, He is a helper.

The Holy Spirit, whom the Father will send in my name, will teach you all things and bring to your remembrance all that has been said to you.

The responsibility as a minister and evangelist can seem overwhelming, but my travels reveal that it comes with countless rewards. The many adventures in my life over the years have been invigorating. I am the richer for having met so many extraordinary people, touched the faces of babies, and shook hands with many dignitaries. I have enjoyed the journey. Writing my story brought back many fond memories and a feeling of gratitude for so many who were there along the way. It has been an adventurous undertaking that began in my birthplace—the island of Colon, our home, where Jeronima and I ate tasty, syrupy fruit and drank coconut juice together, cried 'alligator' tears, unnerved our peers, and bonded in our childish chatter.

Jeronima remains my best friend. She, that little, wide-eyed, adventurous girl who would deliberately dive into gloomy waters of the seacoast after Pluto, was always a very daring survivor. She inherited Lorline's gallantry and resilience. Somehow, we have both miraculously braved our turbulent journey, not only finding strength, but perfecting our self-worth and embracing our purpose. I am so proud to say that she has emerged as a highly anointed woman, loving God and building an exemplary family and ministry. Hallelujah!!!

My sister always desired a happy family and God granted it to her and in return, she gives of her time unselfishly to others. She is married to a kindhearted man who is a pastor. I gained an extraordinary brother-in-law when she and Edgar got together. She and her husband serve in various capacities in their church, including as marriage counselors and Sunday school teachers. With a zeal to see other families whole, my dear sister still evangelizes in various provinces in Panama. She leads the Outreach Ministries, supporting and encouraging women who are broken, depressed, and discouraged. I have been like those women many times in my life.

Jeronima and Edgar have two extremely gifted children: my beautiful niece, Esther and my nephew Abraham, who have inherited the appreciation of music from their 'contralto voice' grandmother. They are also grandparents, exerting a lot of energy with a bouncy two-year-old girl, Faith. This is not unlike my engagement with my precious Vashti, my first grandchild. It is an indescribable joy to see our children grown and doing extraordinarily well.

Each of us can see our mother's astonishing gifts emerging in their lives, especially in my own "special girl" Vonnetta, who is a skilled, self-trained pencil artist. She may one day be famous. My boys are George and Alonso. I am so proud of all their accomplishments. They are strong like their father and exceptionally creative like me. They are both expert tattoo artists and have worked with many well-known people. Mama Lorline would have liked that, having been an entertainer herself in the Caribbean. They are all amazing. Looking back I can now see how consistently the Holy Spirit walked alongside me and my sister.

Chapter 17

My Missionary Trip to Panama

Even though I am from Panama, the Lord sent me back on several occasions to minister there. Here is one of the accounts of the move of the Holy Spirit.

A few years ago, I travelled back home for vacation, arriving on a Saturday afternoon. When I got to my sister's home, my brother-in-law, who was the assistant pastor of the church, informed me that the church was in convocation that week, and that Saturday evening would be the last night of it. The family was already getting dressed for the event, but he turned and pointed to me saying, "You are going to minister tonight!" I was in shock and looked at him with a querying look, wondering what I would do or say. Do you know what he did? He simply walked away with a look on his face as if to say, "You are on your own!"

Guess what I did next? I said, "Lord help me; I have nothing prepared." I had no time to prepare a message, because I had just arrived that afternoon. Well! This was God's response to me: "Let your testimonies ring!" I felt very joyful, because I knew that was easy!

Prior to my trip, the Lord had shown me a vision in which I was ministering at a church service, and as I ministered, I saw people running to the altar confessing their faults and crying out in repentance of their sins. In this vision the altar was filled from corner to corner. The

Lord began to explain to me what I was seeing. He said, "While you are yet speaking, the people will run to the altar for forgiveness of sins and to make things right in their lives."

Part two of the vision: I saw myself sitting in the pew after I finished ministering, and someone came and tapped me on the shoulder and handed me a letter-size white envelope. I figured it was an offering. I tell you the truth, God is an amazing God!

To get back to my story. Here we are at the convocation that Saturday night and I am ready to share or let my testimonies ring. I began by sharing, and the Lord instructed me on what to say. The topic was on fornication, adultery and the lack of faithfulness to the Lord. The delivery of the message was forceful and I stressed the importance of not playing with God by privately committing sexual immorality and then coming to church acting innocently. I even assured the people that men will crawl into congregations and lead silly weak women astray. I intentionally reiterated those words, and suddenly I saw a man who was seated at the back of the church take flight. I was not aware of who he was until later on, when they informed me that he had been frequenting their services trying to seduce the young girls. They said after that night he never came back. Hallelujah!

I tell you the truth! Every detail in my vision was true; because while I was ministering the people were running from everywhere in the congregation to the altar screaming, 'I repent' and saying such things as, 'I am living with this woman for so many years and not married!' Young boys and girls who were fornicating came up to me saying, 'my boyfriend and I are sleeping together.'

There was a mighty move of the Holy Ghost.

Chapter 18

The Holy Spirit:
The Same Yesterday, Today, Forever

The Holy Spirit is the third Person of the Trinity. He is part of God's Personhood; we have God the Father, God the Son, and God the Holy Spirit. He was sent down from Heaven to be our helper.

Even though the Holy Spirit is Deity, He is a Friend; our Comforter. He is the One who was sent to help us. He is always with us. He speaks and makes His presence known. He is not a figment of our imagination, but is very real! To me, the Holy Spirit is a lovely Person; a friend to the friendless. The Holy Spirit is so enjoyable!

I have experienced His presence, His companionship. He is a companion to those who need a friend and He reminds us of the things that Jesus said while He was on earth.

The Holy Spirit is also known as Helper. A helper is one who is there to stand by to assist you. One who will never leave or abandon you under any circumstance. He strengthens us in our weaknesses. He is an intercessor (when we don't know what to pray, the Holy Spirit helps us pray).

The Holy Spirit is a Paraclete, which means one who is called to one's side, who walks shoulder to shoulder with you. He is the Comforter, Counselor, the Spirit of Truth, and Teacher.

He is always present. He is omnipresent; therefore, we must entertain Him; recognize and acknowledge His presence.

He will impart into our lives the ways of righteousness, faithfulness, kindness, compassion, love, wisdom, and much more, enabling us to recognize how glorious, how Holy, how powerful, and available He is.

He is more than our words could ever describe. We cannot comprehend, discover, or even tap into His awesomeness.

He, like our Father God and the Lord Jesus Christ, champions us through life; He is the same yesterday, today, and forever.

PRAISE BE TO GOD
FOR HIS UNSPEAKABLE GIFT.

God Bless You!

In Gratitude

It is with much gratitude, pleasure and delight that I ink my pen to write a memoire in this book written by my sister, Lourdes Lewin.

We, the generation of the Lewin family: Batiste, Nicolas and Jordan, are honored to recognize and appreciate the gift that God has given you to bless many people around the globe.

Reverend Mario E. Nicolas Batiste
August 3, 2021 at 4:25 pm

BIOGRAPHY

LOURDES LEWIN

Lourdes is a powerhouse. Born in Panama, she is an Evangelist, Intercessor, Prophet, Teacher and currently a member of Restoration Church of Jesus Christ Apostolic International, Inc. in Brooklyn, New York, under the leadership of Dr. Roberto Robinson Sr. and First Lady Dr. Monica Robinson.

She has traveled on missionary trips to Hawaii, Holland, Jamaica West Indies, Mexico, Nicaragua, Panama, Trinidad and Tobago, and the Virgin Islands, and she has witnessed the power of God working through her and others.

She is an entrepreneur, who likes to encourage other entrepreneurs by sponsoring Christian Expos as an opportunity to showcase their business. Lourdes continues to shine in the Christian community by helping the poor, feeding the hungry, and winning souls for Christ.

ETERNAL CREATIONS

For more information

Contact Lourdes Lewin
eternalcreationsjcml@yahoo.com

www.ingramcontent.com/pod-product-compliance
Lightning Source LLC
Chambersburg PA
CBHW070928160426
43193CB00011B/1614